The American Collection:
COUNTRY
HOMES

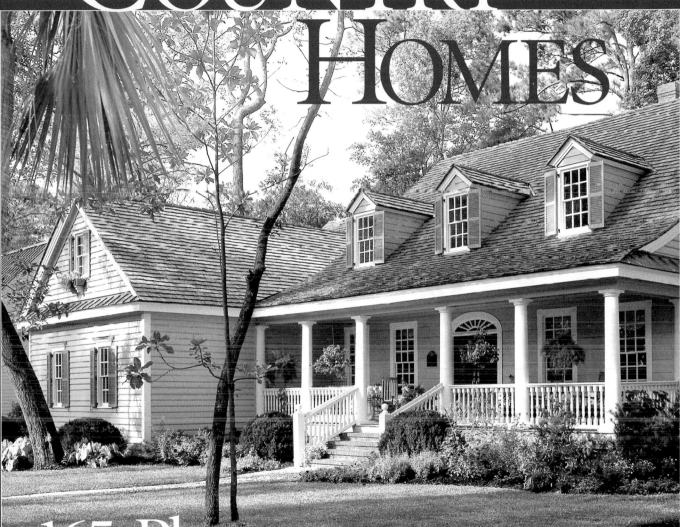

165 Plans With Rural Character

The American Collection:
COUNTRY HOMES

Published by Hanley Wood
One Thomas Circle, NW, Suite 600
Washington, DC 20005

Distribution Center
29333 Lorie Lane
Wixom, Michigan 48393

Group Vice President, General Manager, Andrew Schultz
Editor-in-Chief, Linda Bellamy
Managing Editor, Jason D. Vaughan
Senior Editor, Nate Ewell
Associate Editor, Simon Hyoun
Senior Plan Merchandiser, Morenci C. Clark
Plan Merchandiser, Nicole Phipps
Proofreader/Copywriter, Dyana Weis
Graphic Artist, Joong Min
Plan Data Team Leader, Ryan Emge
Production Manager, Brenda McClary

Vice President, Retail Sales, Scott Hill
National Sales Manager, Bruce Holmes
Director, Plan Products, Matt Higgins

For direct sales, contact Retail Vision at (800) 381-1288 ext 6053

BIG DESIGNS, INC.
President, Creative Director, Anthony D'Elia
Vice President, Business Manager, Megan D'Elia
Vice President, Design Director, Chris Bonavita
Editorial Director, John Roach
Assistant Editor, Tricia Starkey
Senior Art Director, Stephen Reinfurt
Production Director, David Barbella
Photo Editor, Christine DiVuolo
Graphic Designer, Mary Ellen Mulshine
Graphic Designer, Jacque Young
Graphic Designer, Maureen Waters
Assistant Photo Editor, David Halpin
Assistant Production Manager, Rich Fuentes

PHOTO CREDITS
Front Cover: Design HPK0700074, for details, see page 85.
Photos courtesy of William E. Poole Designs, Inc., Islands of Beaufort, Beaufort, S.C.
Back Cover: Design HPK07000007, for details, see page 16. Photos ©1993 Donald A. Gardner Architects, Inc.,
Photography courtesy of Donald A. Gardner Architects, Inc.

10 9 8 7 6 5 4 3 2 1

Printed in the United States of America

Library of Congress Control Number: 2004116171

ISBN: 1-931131-35-X

The American Collection:
COUNTRY HOMES

©1993 DONALD A. GARDNER ARCHITECTS, INC. ; PHOTOGRAPHY COURTESY OF DONALD A. GARDNER ARCHITECTS, INC. ; BOTTOM: PHOTO COURTESY OF: WILLIAM E. POOLE DESIGNS, INC. · ISLANDS OF BEAUFORT, BEAUFORT, SC

hanley▲wood
Passageway

ONLINE EXTRA

Go to:
www.hanleywoodbooks.com/accountryhomes
for access to the Hanley Wood Passageway,
your passage to bonus home plans, bonus articles, online ordering, and more!

Features of this site include:
- A dynamic link that lets you search and
  view bonus home plans
- Online-related feature articles
- Built-in tools to save and view your
  favorite home plans
- A dynamic web link that allows you to
  order your home plan online
- Contact details for the Hanley Wood
  Home Plan Hotline
- Free subscriptions for Hanley Wood
  Home Plan e-news

COUNTRY CHARM

I n one context, the word "country" is synonymous with "nation." When looking at country architecture, that's a telling comparison, since country homes in many ways have become the most American style of home.

As the earliest settlers moved across the continent, they found vast expanses to establish their new homes. From those earliest country homes to the ones built today, we find a mix of architectural influences, but consistent ideals—an appreciation of the outdoors, a welcoming, comfortable appeal, and enough space for the whole family.

Right top: The decorative touches of the Victorian era make Design HPK0700127 stand out. For more, see page 139. Right bottom: Craftsman styling gives Design HPK0700055 a rustic appeal, but the interior is thoroughly modern. See page 65 for details.

With their beautiful country settings, it's no surprise that these homes connect so well to their surroundings. That connection can take many forms—from sprawling front porches to the use of large picture windows—but there's no doubt that this association with nature is as much a part of a great country home as its walls or roof.

A country home doesn't need a breathtaking view to take advantage of the outdoors, either. Something as simple as a screened porch or a convenient deck can expand your living space tremendously and ease the transition between indoors and out.

How a home fits with its surroundings helps establish its welcoming character, as well. Even the largest country homes seem to call guests towards them as they approach, unlike so many luxury homes that project a cold, impersonal facade.

Inside, that comforting feeling continues in the layout and decor of the best country homes. Rooms connect with each other easily to bring everyone together, and family treasures and photos lend a personal touch that even a fine work of art simply cannot match.

That personal touch and spirit of family can be seen most clearly when relatives gather for the holidays or on vacation—the times when country homes are at their best. Plan your country home accordingly, with plenty of space to host family events in the future.

The styles in this book showcase the variety of country homes found across America. From the simple lines of a farmhouse or cottage to the intricate details found in a Victorian or Craftsman home, each has something that's distinct to the countryside. As broad as the range of country homes is, there's still something unmistakable about each one that shows it clearly belongs in rural America.

Whether you live in the country or just want to feel like you do, the designs in this book will help you bring the country spirit to your home. ∎

OPEN AIR

There's a feeling of Old Charleston in this stately home—particularly in the quiet side porch, which wraps around the kitchen and breakfast rooms. The heart of this home is the spacious central great room, which features a welcoming fireplace and a wall of windows with wide views of the rear property. Nearby, the breakfast bay allows access to both the rear covered porch and the wraparound porch. The front of the plan provides a formal room that can easily serve as a parlor, study or dining room. All of the first-floor rooms offer views to the garden in back. Upstairs, two additional bedrooms share a full bath and a private hall that leads to a guest suite.

plan# HPK0700001

Style: Country Cottage
First Floor: 1,804 sq. ft.
Second Floor: 1,041sq. ft.
Total: 2,845 sq. ft.
Bedrooms: 4
Bathrooms: 3½
Width: 57' - 3"
Depth: 71' - 0"
Foundation: Finished
Walkout Basement

SEARCH ONLINE @ EPLANS.COM

REAR EXTERIOR

A bold exterior creates an impressive but welcoming feel as you approach the home (opposite page). Simple elegance and views of the front property highlight the dining room (above left). A stacked-stone fireplace and honey-hued floors add rustic glow to the great room (above right). Refreshing garden views will be enjoyed from the great room and rear porch (left).

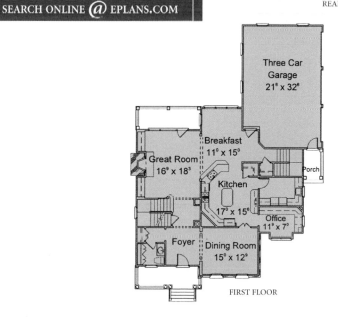

FIRST FLOOR

Three Car Garage
21⁶ x 32⁶

Breakfast
11⁹ x 15⁰

Great Room
16⁹ x 18³

Kitchen
17⁰ x 15⁶

Porch

Office
11⁸ x 7⁰

Foyer

Dining Room
15⁰ x 12⁹

SECOND FLOOR

Bedroom #4
15⁸ x 16³

Master Bedroom
15⁹ x 23³

Master Bath

Study Area

WIC

Bedroom #2
11⁹ x 14⁶

Bedroom #3
13⁰ x 12⁰

EXTERIOR PHOTOGRAPH BY DAN TYRPAK, INTERIOR PHOTOGRAPHY BY BOB GREENSPAN

RUSTIC CHARM

This rustic Craftsman home combines an earthy stone-and-siding facade with a luxurious floor plan for a wonderful home that will please everyone. The great room greets family and friends with a stone hearth and French doors to the rear deck. With an enormous walk-in pantry and a butler's pantry with a wine niche off the dining room, the vaulted kitchen is ready for entertaining. In the master bedroom, a vaulted ceiling and French doors add simple elegance; the bath pampers with a spa tub and block-glass encased shower. A nearby den offers seclusion, the perfect place to retreat with a good book.

Step downstairs and find a space that epitomizes the comfort of country living. The game room is a warm space that feels cozy despite its impressive size. Best of all, it features something for everyone: a fireplace, built-in media center, space for a pool table or children's games, and a wet bar and wine cellar. The laundry room is nearby as well, easy to serve the three downstairs bedrooms, and has room for hobbies.

Skillfully blended exterior materials give this home a unique charm (opposite page). Honey-toned woods and wrought-iron furnishings coupled with a tiled backsplash create a rustic atmosphere in the kitchen (above left). Light floods the eat-in kitchen, with a deck just steps away for outdoor dining (below).

A towering stone hearth serves as the focal point of the stunning great room (above left). The master suite includes two vanities, and plenty of space for cabinets and all the storage shelves you could ask for (above right). In the luxurious master bedroom, which features a soaring vaulted ceiling, natural light from the tall arched window complements the golden and brown tones of the decor (left).

MAIN LEVEL

LOWER LEVEL

plan# HPK0700002

Style: European Cottage
Main Level: 2,602 sq. ft.
Lower Level: 2,440 sq. ft.
Total: 5,042 sq. ft.
Bedrooms: 4
Bathrooms: 4½ + ½
Width: 88' - 0"
Depth: 50' - 0"
Foundation: Finished
Walkout Basement

SEARCH ONLINE @ EPLANS.COM

ORDER BLUEPRINTS 24 HOURS, 7 DAYS A WEEK, AT 1-800-521-6797

ON THE FARM

America was, at its roots, an agrarian society, and large stretches of the country remain reliant on farming today. It's a profession that helped to define us as a nation, and not surprisingly led to a unique form of architecture. Whether captured in the background of Grant Wood's iconic painting, American Gothic, or seen through car windows while driving down long country roads, farmhouses help define our landscape and our consciousness.

Large farmhouse front porches offer a place for a swing, or a spot to survey the fields. In a film like Field of Dreams, it was also a place from which to watch baseball, the most American of sports.

The connection to the land doesn't end with the porch. Farmhouses are typically built with wood, and designed to blend in with their surroundings, even if the tallest thing within acres is a cornstalk.

Inside you'll find plenty of space for the family, as the large two-story designs offer a number of upstairs bedrooms. Today's farmhouse plans often move the master suite to the main level for convenience, opening upstairs to possibilities like a media room or a two-story great room.■

This gorgeous farmhouse, with touches of Colonial and Greek Revival styling, features an inviting front porch and a deck in back. For details on Design HPK0700023, see page 32.

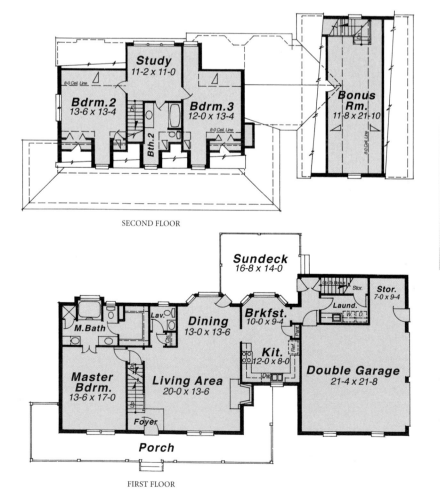

Study
11-2 x 11-0

Bdrm.2
13-6 x 13-4

Bdrm.3
12-0 x 13-4

8-0 Ceil. Line

Bth.2

Bonus Rm.
11-8 x 21-10

SECOND FLOOR

Sundeck
16-8 x 14-0

M.Bath

Lav.

Dining
13-0 x 13-6

Brkfst.
10-0 x 9-4

Laund.

Stor.
7-0 x 9-4

Kit.
12-0 x 8-0

Master Bdrm.
13-6 x 17-0

Living Area
20-0 x 13-6

Double Garage
21-4 x 21-8

Foyer

Porch

FIRST FLOOR

plan# HPK0700003

Style: Farmhouse
First Floor: 1,362 sq. ft.
Second Floor: 729 sq. ft.
Total: 2,091 sq. ft.
Bonus Space: 384 sq. ft.
Bedrooms: 3
Bathrooms: 2½
Width: 72' - 0"
Depth: 38' - 0"
Foundation: Unfinished Basement, Slab, Crawlspace

SEARCH ONLINE @ EPLANS.COM

This design's open flow leads you through the living room to the dining room, where access through the bay opens to a sun deck. A kitchen connects to a bayed breakfast area. The master bedroom features a master bath suite with all the amenities. The second floor provides two spacious bedrooms with a shared study or computer room.

plan# HPK0700004

Style: Farmhouse
Square Footage: 1,864
Bonus Space: 420 sq. ft.
Bedrooms: 3
Bathrooms: 2½
Width: 71' - 0"
Depth: 56' - 4"

SEARCH ONLINE @ EPLANS.COM

Quaint and cozy on the outside with porches front and back, this three-bedroom country home surprises with an open floor plan featuring a large great room with a cathedral ceiling. The privately located master suite has a cathedral ceiling and access to the deck. Two secondary bedrooms share a full hall bath. A bonus room makes expanding easy.

REAR EXTERIOR

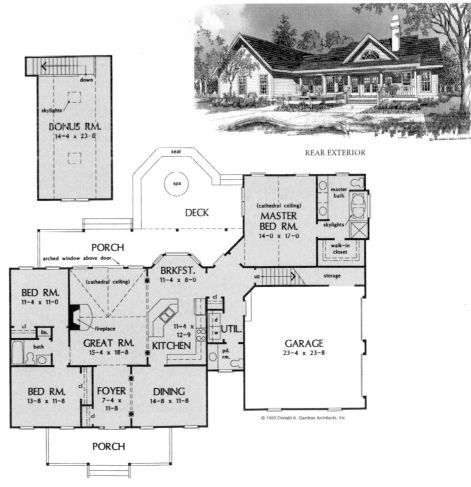

Multipane windows, country siding, and a wide, welcoming front porch come together to create this charming farmhouse. Inside, the kitchen flows effortlessly into the bayed breakfast nook and formal dining room. The two-story great room features a fireplace and rear-porch access through French doors. The first-floor master suite is graced with a tray ceiling, relaxing bath, and French-door access to the rear porch. Upstairs, three bedrooms and a bonus room provide space for the whole family.

plan# HPK0700005

Style: Farmhouse
First Floor: 1,798 sq. ft.
Second Floor: 723 sq. ft.
Total: 2,521 sq. ft.
Bonus Space: 349 sq. ft.
Bedrooms: 4
Bathrooms: 3½
Width: 66' - 8"
Depth: 49' - 8"

SEARCH ONLINE @ EPLANS.COM

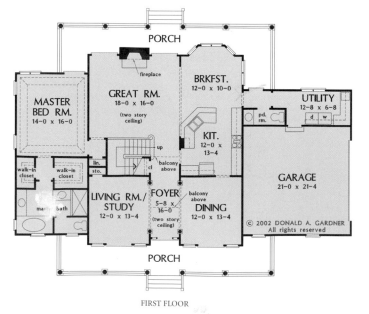

FIRST FLOOR

SECOND FLOOR

plan # HPK0700006

Style: Country Cottage
First Floor: 2,086 sq. ft.
Second Floor: 1,077 sq. ft.
Total: 3,163 sq. ft.
Bonus Space: 403 sq. ft.
Bedrooms: 4
Bathrooms: 3½
Width: 81' - 10"
Depth: 51' - 8"

SEARCH ONLINE @ EPLANS.COM

This beautiful farmhouse, with its prominent twin gables and bays, has just the right amount of country style. The master suite is quietly tucked away downstairs with no rooms directly above. The family cook will love the spacious U-shaped kitchen and adjoining bayed breakfast nook. A bonus room awaits expansion on the second floor, where three large bedrooms share two full baths.

REAR EXTERIOR

SECOND FLOOR

FIRST FLOOR

REAR EXTERIOR

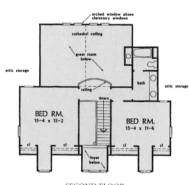

SECOND FLOOR

plan# HPK0700007

Style: Farmhouse
First Floor: 2,316 sq. ft.
Second Floor: 721 sq. ft.
Total: 3,037 sq. ft.
Bonus Space: 545 sq. ft.
Bedrooms: 4
Bathrooms: 3½
Width: 95' - 4"
Depth: 54' - 10"

SEARCH ONLINE @ EPLANS.COM

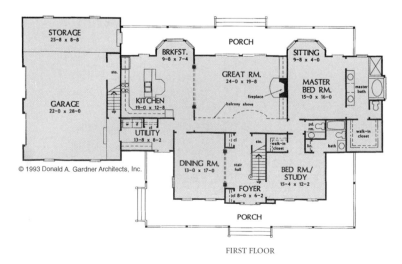

© 1993 Donald A. Gardner Architects, Inc.

FIRST FLOOR

The entrance to this farmhouse enjoys a Palladian clerestory window, lending an abundance of natural light to the foyer. The great room furthers this feeling of airiness with a balcony above and two sets of sliding glass doors leading to the back porch. For privacy, the master suite occupies the right side of the first floor.

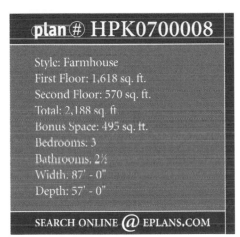

plan # HPK0700008

Style: Farmhouse
First Floor: 1,618 sq. ft.
Second Floor: 570 sq. ft.
Total: 2,188 sq. ft.
Bonus Space: 495 sq. ft.
Bedrooms: 3
Bathrooms: 2½
Width: 87' - 0"
Depth: 57' - 0"

SEARCH ONLINE @ EPLANS.COM

The foyer and great room enjoy

Palladian clerestory windows, which allow natural light to enter the well-planned interior of this country home. The spacious great room boasts a fireplace and built-in cabinets. The kitchen has a cooktop island counter and is placed conveniently between the breakfast room and the formal dining room. A generous first-floor master suite offers plenty of closet space and a lavish bath. Upstairs, two family bedrooms share a full bath. Bonus space over the garage awaits later development.

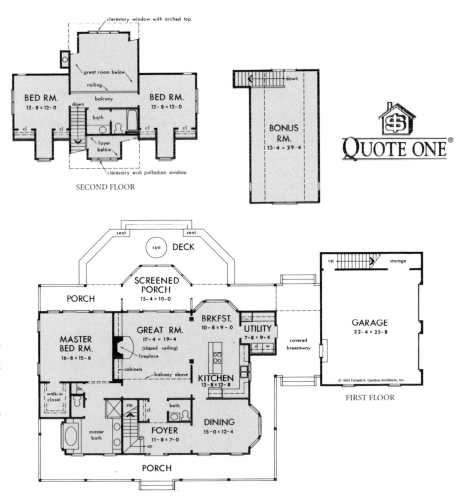

SECOND FLOOR

BONUS RM.
15-4 × 29-4

QUOTE ONE®

FIRST FLOOR

Filled with the charm of farmhouse details, such as twin gables and bay windows, this design begins with a classic covered porch. The entry leads to a foyer flanked by columns that separate it from the formal dining and living rooms. The U-shaped kitchen separates the dining room from the bayed breakfast room. The first-floor master suite features a bedroom with a tray ceiling and a luxurious private bath.

plan# HPK0700009

Style: Farmhouse
First Floor: 1,914 sq. ft.
Second Floor: 597 sq. ft.
Total: 2,511 sq. ft.
Bonus Space: 487 sq. ft.
Bedrooms: 3
Bathrooms: 2½
Width: 79' - 2"
Depth: 51' - 6"

SEARCH ONLINE @ EPLANS.COM

FIRST FLOOR

SECOND FLOOR

ORDER BLUEPRINTS 24 HOURS, 7 DAYS A WEEK, AT 1-800-521-6797

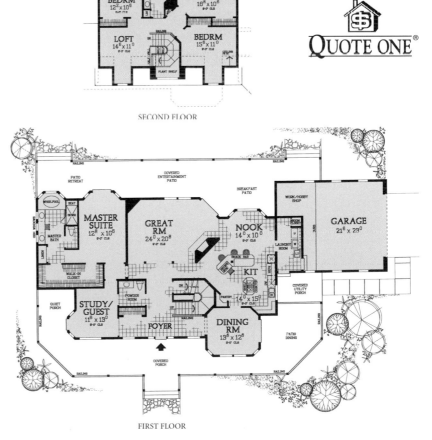

SECOND FLOOR

FIRST FLOOR

plan(#) HPK0700010

L

Style: Farmhouse
First Floor: 2,347 sq. ft.
Second Floor: 1,087 sq. ft.
Total: 3,434 sq. ft.
Bedrooms: 4
Bathrooms: 2½
Width: 93' - 6"
Depth: 61' - 0"
Foundation: Unfinished Basement

SEARCH ONLINE @ EPLANS.COM

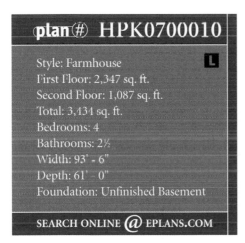

QUOTE ONE®

Dutch-gable rooflines and a gabled wraparound porch provide an extra measure of farmhouse style to this lovely plan. The foyer opens to the study or guest bedroom on the left that leads to the master suite. The kitchen combines with the great room, the breakfast nook, and the dining room for entertaining options. A loft and three family bedrooms inhabit the second floor.

Wood siding, muntin window dormers, and a double-decker porch exemplify Southern country style in this welcoming plan. Slide off your porch swing and enter through the foyer, flanked by the bayed living room and dining room. The family room flows effortlessly into the breakfast area and the kitchen, complete with an island. The master bedroom wows with a closet designed for a true clotheshorse. Three upstairs bedrooms enjoy access to the upper porch and space for a future recreation room.

ptan# HPK0700011

Style: Farmhouse
First Floor: 1,995 sq. ft.
Second Floor: 1,062 sq. ft.
Total: 3,057 sq. ft.
Bonus Space: 459 sq. ft.
Bedrooms: 4
Bathrooms: 3½
Width: 71' - 0"
Depth: 57' - 4"
Foundation: Unfinished Basement

SEARCH ONLINE @ EPLANS.COM

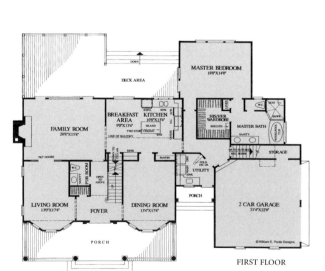

FIRST FLOOR

SECOND FLOOR

plan # HPK0700012

LD

Style: Country Cottage
First Floor: 1,752 sq. ft.
Second Floor: 906 sq. ft.
Total: 2,658 sq. ft.
Bedrooms: 4
Bathrooms: 3½
Width: 74' - 0"
Depth: 51' - 7"
Foundation: Unfinished Basement

SEARCH ONLINE @ EPLANS.COM

Delightfully proportioned and outwardly symmetrical, this Victorian farm-house has lots of curb appeal. Archways, display niches, and columns help define the great room, which offers a fireplace framed by windows. A formal parlor and a dining room flank the reception hall, and each offers a bay window. The master suite boasts two sets of French doors to the wraparound porch. Upstairs, three bedrooms—or two and a den—and two full baths complete the plan.

QUOTE ONE®

FIRST FLOOR

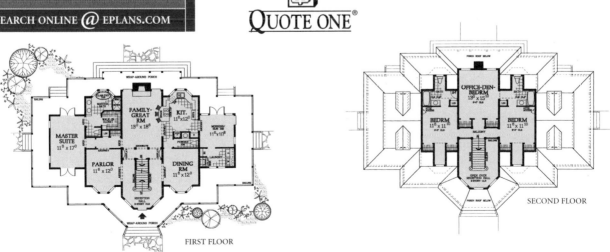

SECOND FLOOR

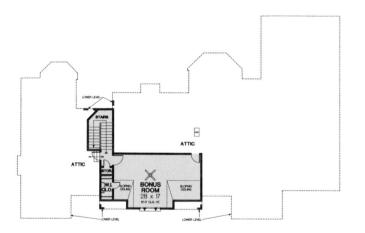

plan# HPK0700013

Style: Farmhouse
Square Footage: 3,439
Bonus Space: 514 sq. ft.
Bedrooms: 4
Bathrooms: 3½
Width: 100' - 0"
Depth: 67' - 11"
Foundation: Crawlspace, Slab, Unfinished Basement

SEARCH ONLINE @ EPLANS.COM

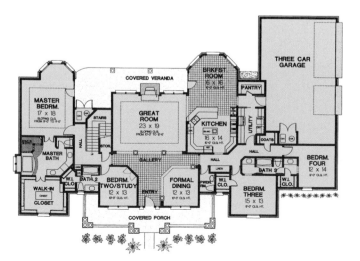

This country farmhouse really stands out with its steep roof gable, shuttered muntin windows, stone siding, and double-columned front porch. Inside, the great room provides an impressive fireplace and overlooks the rear veranda. The island kitchen opens to a bayed breakfast room. The right side of the home includes a utility room, a three-car garage, and two family bedrooms that share a bath. The master wing of the home enjoys a bayed sitting area, a sumptuous bath, and an enormous walk-in closet.

plan # HPK0700014

Style: Farmhouse
Square Footage: 2,539
Bonus Space: 636 sq. ft.
Bedrooms: 4
Bathrooms: 3
Width: 98' - 0"
Depth: 53' - 11"
Foundation: Slab

SEARCH ONLINE @ EPLANS.COM

Rustic corner quoins, a covered front porch, and interesting gables give this home its classic country character. The entry opens to the formal living areas that include a large dining room to the right, and straight ahead to a spacious living room warmed by a fireplace. Casual meals can be enjoyed overlooking the covered veranda and rear grounds from the connecting breakfast room. The other side of the gallery accesses the luxurious master suite and three secondary bedrooms—all with walk-in closets.

plan# HPK0700015

L | D

Style: Farmhouse
Square Footage: 2,090
Bedrooms: 3
Bathrooms: 2½
Width: 84' - 6"
Depth: 64' - 0"
Foundation: Crawlspace

SEARCH ONLINE @ EPLANS.COM

This classic farmhouse enjoys a wraparound porch that's perfect for enjoyment of the outdoors. The formal dining room is defined by a low wall and graceful archways set off by decorative columns. The tiled kitchen has a center island counter with a snack bar and adjoins a laundry area. Two family bedrooms reside to the side of the plan; each enjoys private access to the covered porch. A secluded master suite features a sitting area with access to the rear terrace and spa.

plan # HPK0700016

Style: Farmhouse
First Floor. 1,008 sq. ft.
Second Floor: 917 sq. ft.
Total: 1,925 sq. ft.
Bedrooms: 3
Bathrooms: 2½
Width: 56' - 0"
Depth: 36' - 0"
Foundation: Crawlspace,
Unfinished Basement

SEARCH ONLINE @ EPLANS.COM

Tradition in symmetry is repre-
sented in the clean lines and attractive front
porch of this country home. Inside, the two-
story foyer is flanked by a formal living room
and a more casual great room. Two sun rooms
echo each other at opposite ends of the home.
Upstairs, a master bedroom features a private
fireplace and sumptuous bath. Two secondary
bedrooms and a hall bath complete this level.

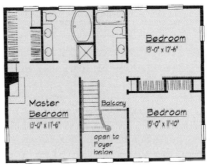

SECOND FLOOR

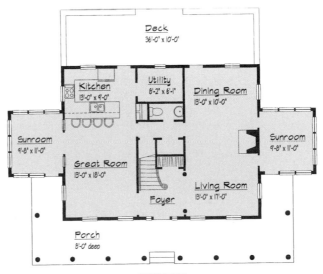

FIRST FLOOR

SECOND FLOOR

plan# HPK0700017

Style: Farmhouse
First Floor: 1,913 sq. ft.
Second Floor: 997 sq. ft.
Total: 2,910 sq. ft.
Bonus Space: 377 sq. ft.
Bedrooms: 4
Bathrooms: 3½
Width: 63' - 0"
Depth: 59' - 4"
Foundation: Crawlspace,
Unfinished Basement

SEARCH ONLINE @ EPLANS.COM

FIRST FLOOR

This enchanting farmhouse brings the past to life with plenty of modern amenities. An open-flow kitchen/breakfast area and family room combination is the heart of the home, opening up to the screened porch and enjoying the warmth of a fireplace. For more formal occasions, the foyer is flanked by a living room on the left and a dining room on the right. An elegant master bedroom, complete with a super-size walk-in closet, is tucked away quietly behind the garage. Three more bedrooms reside upstairs, along with two full baths and a future recreation room.

plan# HPK0700018

Style: Southern Colonial
First Floor: 1,273 sq. ft.
Second Floor: 1,358 sq. ft.
Total: 2,631 sq. ft.
Bedrooms: 4
Bathrooms: 3½
Width: 54' - 10"
Depth: 48' - 6"
Foundation: Crawlspace

SEARCH ONLINE @ EPLANS.COM

This two-story home suits the needs of each household member. Family gatherings won't be crowded in the spacious family room, which is adjacent to the kitchen and the break-fast area. Just beyond the foyer, the dining and living rooms view the front yard. The master suite features its own full bath with dual vani-ties, a whirlpool tub, and separate shower. Three family bedrooms—one with a walk-in closet—and two full hall baths are available upstairs. Extra storage space is found in the two-car garage.

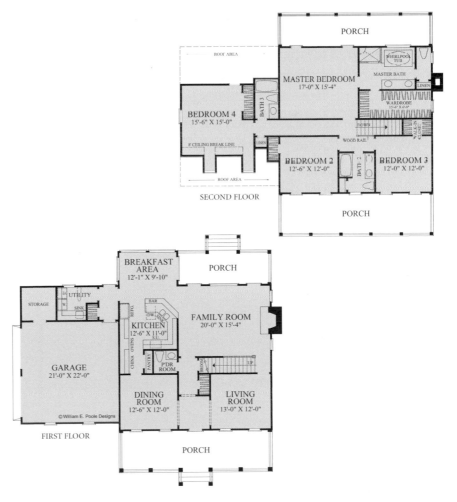

Beginning with the interest of a wraparound porch, there's a feeling of country charm in this two-story plan. Formal dining and living rooms, visible from the entry, offer ample space for gracious entertaining. The large family room is truly a place of warmth and welcome with its gorgeous bay window, fireplace, and French doors to the living room. Upstairs, the secondary bedrooms share an efficient compartmented bath. The expansive master suite has its own luxury bath with a double vanity, whirlpool tub, walk-in closet, and dressing area.

plan # HPK0700019

Style: Farmhouse
First Floor: 1,188 sq. ft.
Second Floor: 1,172 sq. ft.
Total: 2,360 sq. ft.
Bedrooms: 4
Bathrooms: 2½
Width: 58' - 0"
Depth: 40' - 0"

SEARCH ONLINE @ EPLANS.COM

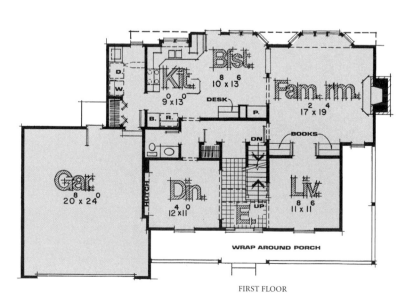

FIRST FLOOR

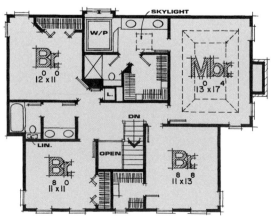

SECOND FLOOR

ORDER BLUEPRINTS 24 HOURS, 7 DAYS A WEEK, AT 1-800-521-6797

plan(#) HPK0700020

Style: Farmhouse
First Floor: 1,322 sq. ft.
Second Floor: 1,272 sq. ft.
Total: 2,594 sq. ft.
Bonus Space: 80 sq. ft.
Bedrooms: 4
Bathrooms: 2½
Width: 56' 0"
Depth: 48' 0"

SEARCH ONLINE @ EPLANS.COM

Here's the luxury you've been looking for—

from the wraparound covered front porch to the bright sun room off the breakfast room. A sunken family room with a fireplace serves everyday casual gatherings, while the more formal living and dining rooms are reserved for special entertaining situations. The kitchen features a central island with a snack bar. Upstairs are four bedrooms, including a lovely master suite with French doors to the private bath. Double vanities in the shared bath easily serve the three family bedrooms.

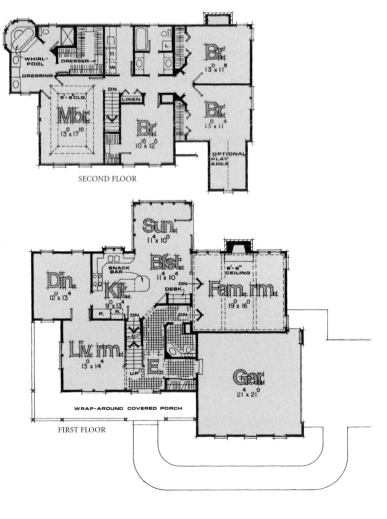

SECOND FLOOR

FIRST FLOOR

SECOND FLOOR

SHWR.

LINEN

W.i.c.

Vltd. M.Bath

PLANT SHELF ABOVE

Bedroom 3
11^0 x 11^6

W.i.c.

Bath

FRENCH DOOR

TRAY CLG.

Master Suite
12^9 x 17^0

STAIRS DN.

OPEN RAIL

Opt. Bonus
17^5 x 13^5

LINEN

Foyer Below

Bedroom 2
13^0 x 11^0

---

plan # HPK0700021

Style: Southern Colonial
First Floor: 1,071 sq. ft.
Second Floor: 924 sq. ft.
Total: 1,995 sq. ft.
Bonus Space: 280 sq. ft.
Bedrooms: 3
Bathrooms: 2½
Width: 55' - 10"
Depth: 38' - 6"
Foundation: Crawlspace, Unfinished Walkout Basement, Slab

SEARCH ONLINE @ EPLANS.COM

Move-up buyers can enjoy all the luxuries of this two-story home highlighted by an angled staircase separating the dining room from casual living areas. A bay window and built-in desk in the breakfast area are just a few of the plan's amenities. The sleeping zone occupies the second floor—away from everyday activities—and includes a master suite and two secondary bedrooms.

FIRST FLOOR

FRENCH DOOR

Breakfast

DESK

FPL.

Family Room
19^0 x 15^0

PANTRY

SERVING BAR

DW.

Kitchen

RANGE

REF.

Living Room
12^9 x 12^2

STAIRS DN.

OPEN RAIL

Pwdr.

Two Story Foyer

COATS

Garage
19^9 x 23^5

Dining Room
13^0 x 11^0

copyright © 1997 frank betz associates, inc.

Covered Porch

ORDER BLUEPRINTS 24 HOURS, 7 DAYS A WEEK, AT 1-800-521-6797

plan# HPK0700022

Style: Country Cottage
First Floor: 1,142 sq. ft.
Second Floor: 1,004 sq. ft.
Total: 2,146 sq. ft.
Bonus Space: 156 sq. ft.
Bedrooms: 4
Bathrooms: 3
Width: 52' - 4"
Depth: 38' - 6"
Foundation: Crawlspace, Slab,
Unfinished Walkout Basement

SEARCH ONLINE @ EPLANS.COM

SECOND FLOOR

This gracious four-bedroom home adds siding, gables, and shutters to a very livable floor plan. Three bedrooms and a bedroom/study, along with three full baths, provide plenty of room for family and guests. A tray ceiling adorns the master bedroom; a vaulted master bath adds to the spaciousness of this private retreat. The two-story family room sits near the kitchen and bayed breakfast area. An optional bonus room is available upstairs for future expansion.

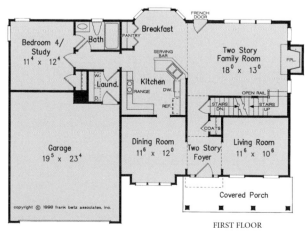

FIRST FLOOR

SECOND FLOOR

FIRST FLOOR

plan # HPK0700023

Style: Farmhouse
First Floor: 1,700 sq. ft.
Second Floor: 1,585 sq. ft.
Total: 3,285 sq. ft.
Bonus Space: 176 sq. ft.
Bedrooms: 5
Bathrooms: 4
Width: 60' - 0"
Depth: 47' - 6"
Foundation: Finished Walkout
Basement

SEARCH ONLINE @ EPLANS.COM

The front porch of this two-story farmhouse opens to a traditional foyer flanked by the formal areas. For casual family living, a great room—with a fireplace—and a kitchen with a breakfast area will serve the family's needs. Upstairs, the master suite contains a bayed sitting area and a private bath. A spacious rear deck complements the inviting front porch in this spacious design.

plan# HPK0700024

Style: Georgian
First Floor: 1,327 sq. ft.
Second Floor: 1,099 sq. ft.
Total: 2,426 sq. ft.
Bonus Space: 290 sq. ft.
Bedrooms: 4
Bathrooms: 3
Width: 54' - 4"
Depth: 42' - 10"
Foundation: Crawlspace, Unfinished Walkout Basement

SEARCH ONLINE @ EPLANS.COM

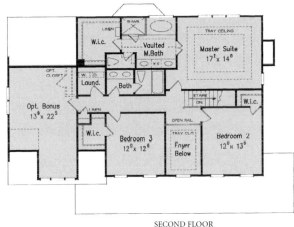

SECOND FLOOR

A Southern classic, this lovely home will become a treasured place to call your own. The entry makes a grand impression; double doors open to the foyer where French doors reveal a study. To the right, the dining room is designed for entertaining with easy access to the angled serving-bar kitchen. A bayed breakfast nook leads into the hearth-warmed family room. Tucked to the rear, a bedroom with a full bath makes an ideal guest room. The master suite is upstairs and enjoys a private vaulted spa bath. Two additional bedrooms reside on this level and join a full bath and an optional bonus room, perfect as a kid's retreat, home gym, or crafts room.

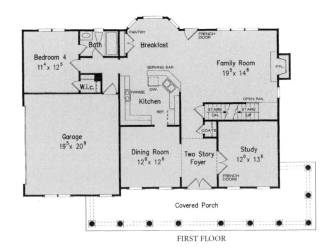

FIRST FLOOR

SECOND FLOOR

plan# HPK0700025

Style: Plantation
First Floor: 2,113 sq. ft.
Second Floor: 2,098 sq. ft.
Total: 4,211 sq. ft.
Bonus Space: 76 sq. ft.
Bedrooms: 5
Bathrooms: 4½
Width: 68' - 6"
Depth: 53' - 0"
Foundation: Slab, Unfinished
Walkout Basement, Crawlspace

SEARCH ONLINE @ EPLANS.COM

FIRST FLOOR

This two-story farmhouse has much to offer, with the most exciting feature being the opulent master suite, which takes up almost the entire width of the upper level. French doors access the large master bedroom with its coffered ceiling. Steps lead to a separate sitting room with a fireplace and sun-filled bay window. On the first floor, an island kitchen and a bayed breakfast room flow into a two-story family room with a raised-hearth fireplace, built-in shelves, and French-door access to the rear yard.

plan # HPK0700026

Style: Southern Colonial
First Floor: 1,141 sq. ft.
Second Floor: 1,202 sq. ft.
Total: 2,343 sq. ft.
Bedrooms: 4
Bathrooms: 2½
Width: 50' 0"
Depth: 49' - 0"
Foundation: Crawlspace, Unfinished Walkout Basement

SEARCH ONLINE @ EPLANS.COM

Step inside this charming traditional home to find a plan with open spaces and wonderful details. The two-story foyer leads into a family room with a rear window wall and a see-through fireplace for a cozy atmosphere. The island kitchen, keeping room, and breakfast nook all enjoy a view of the fireplace. A dining room on the left overlooks the wrap-around porch and would also make a great living room. Upstairs, the master suite celebrates luxury with a vaulted resort bath, immense walk-in closet, and the option to annex Bedroom 4 and create a vaulted sitting room. A two-car garage with convenient storage completes this plan.

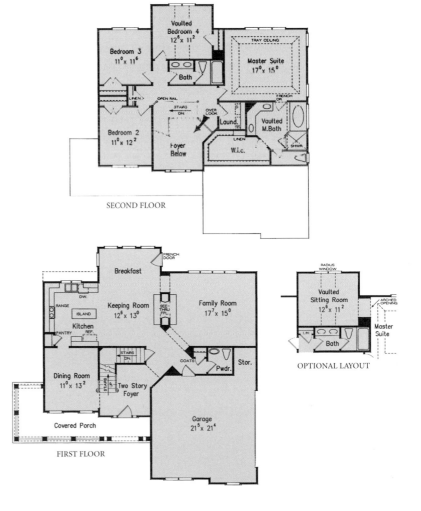

SECOND FLOOR

FIRST FLOOR

OPTIONAL LAYOUT

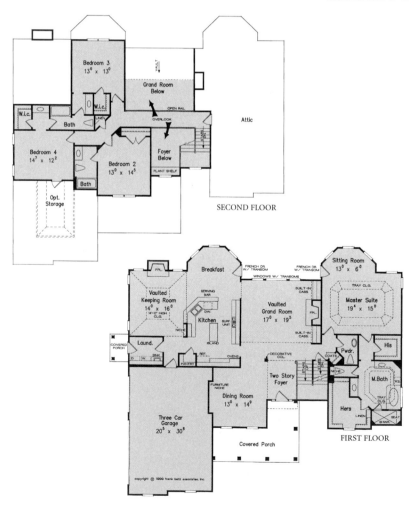

SECOND FLOOR

FIRST FLOOR

plan# HPK0700027

Style: Country Cottage
First Floor: 2,293 sq. ft.
Second Floor: 992 sq. ft.
Total: 3,285 sq. ft.
Bonus Space: 131 sq. ft.
Bedrooms: 4
Bathrooms: 3½
Width: 71' - 0"
Depth: 62' - 0"
Foundation: Crawlspace, Unfinished
Walkout Basement

SEARCH ONLINE @ EPLANS.COM

A combination of stone, siding, and multiple rooflines creates a cottage feel to this large home. Inside, the grand room and keeping room feature fireplaces and vaulted ceilings—the grand room adds built-in cabinets and windows with transoms. A sumptuous master suite enjoys a sitting room, a tray ceiling, and a lavish private bath featuring a shower with a built-in seat. The gourmet kitchen enjoys an island countertop, a serving bar, a walk-in pantry, and access to the three-car garage. Three additional bedrooms are found upstairs with two full baths—Bedrooms 3 and 4 each include large walk-in closets.

plan# HPK0700028

Style: Farmhouse
First Floor: 1,250 sq. ft.
Second Floor: 1,166 sq. ft.
Total: 2,416 sq. ft.
Bedrooms: 4
Bathrooms: 2½
Width: 64' 0"
Depth: 52' - 0"
Foundation: Unfinished Walkout Basement, Unfinished Basement

SEARCH ONLINE @ EPLANS.COM

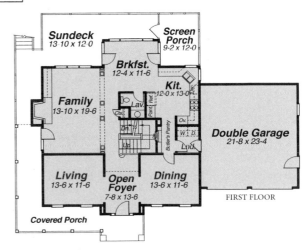

With its classic features, this home is reminiscent of Main Street, USA. The two-story foyer is flanked by the formal living and dining rooms, and the stairs are tucked back in the center of the house. Columns create a separation from the family room to the breakfast area, keeping that open feeling across the entire rear of the house. Corner windows in the kitchen look into the side yard and rear screened porch. The porch leads to the rear deck, which also ties into the side porch, creating outdoor living on three sides of the house. As you ascend the staircase to the second floor, you will pass a lighted panel of stained glass on the landing, creating the illusion of a window wall. The second floor features four bedrooms and a compartmented hall bath.

SECOND FLOOR

Sundeck 9-2 x 12-0
Master Bdrm. 12-4 x 17-6
M.Bath
Bdrm. 4 13-6 x 11-6
Bath 2
Lin.
Storage
Bdrm. 3 13-6 x 11-6
Open Foyer
Bdrm. 2 13-6 x 11-6

FIRST FLOOR

Sundeck 13-10 x 12-0
Screen Porch 9-2 x 12-0
Brkfst. 12-4 x 11-6
Kit. 12-0 x 13-0
Family 13-10 x 19-6
Lav.
Pantry/Ref.
Butler's Pantry
Double Garage 21-8 x 23-4
Living 13-6 x 11-6
Open Foyer 7-8 x 13-6
Dining 13-6 x 11-6
Covered Porch

Dormers and columns decorate the exterior of this three-bedroom country home. Inside, the foyer has immediate access to one family bedroom and the formal dining area. Ahead is the great room with a warming fireplace and ribbon of windows for natural lighting. The master suite is set to the back of the plan and has a lavish bath with a garden tub, separate shower, and two vanities.

plan # HPK0700029

Style: Southern Colonial
Square Footage: 1,688
Bedrooms: 3
Bathrooms: 2
Width: 70' - 1"
Depth: 48' - 0"
Foundation: Crawlspace, Slab, Unfinished Basement

SEARCH ONLINE @ EPLANS.COM

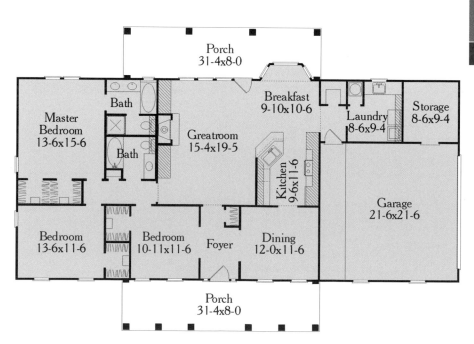

SECOND FLOOR

plan# HPK0700030

Style: Farmhouse
First Floor: 1,152 sq. ft.
Second Floor: 452 sq. ft.
Total: 1,604 sq. ft.
Bonus Space: 115 sq. ft.
Bedrooms: 3
Bathrooms: 2½
Width: 36' - 0"
Depth: 40' - 0"
Foundation: Crawlspace,
Unfinished Basement

SEARCH ONLINE @ EPLANS.COM

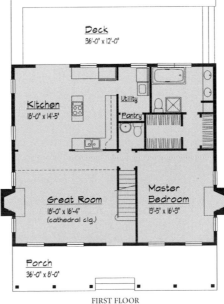

FIRST FLOOR

Three dormers, two chimneys,
and a covered front porch combine to make
this home attractive in any neighborhood.
Inside, a great room greets family and friends
with a cathedral ceiling and a charming fireplace. The master suite boasts a second fireplace, as well as two closets and a private bath.
Upstairs, two secondary bedrooms share a hall
bath and have access to a bonus room.

Colonial style meets farmhouse charm in this plan, furnishing old-fashioned charisma with a flourish. Off the dining room is a large island kitchen that easily serves both formal and informal areas. Nearby is the spacious great room, warmed by a center fireplace and large windows. The secluded master suite, with its vaulted ceiling, is tucked behind the three-car garage. The master bath contains a relaxing tub, double-bowl vanity, separate shower, and compartmented toilet.

plan# HPK0700031

Style: Farmhouse
Square Footage: 2,078
Bedrooms: 4
Bathrooms: 2
Width: 75' - 0"
Depth: 47' - 10"
Foundation: Slab

SEARCH ONLINE @ EPLANS.COM

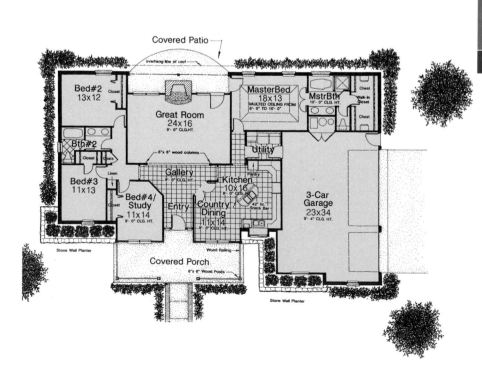

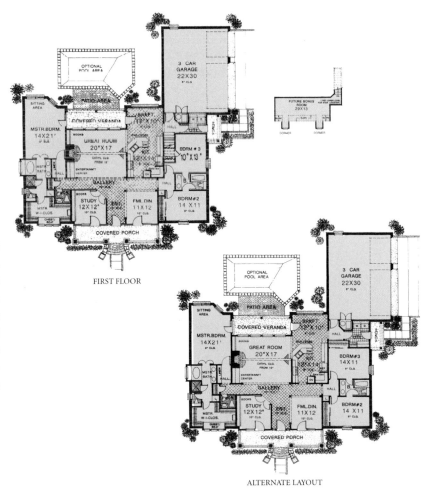

plan # HPK0700032

Style: Farmhouse
Square Footage: 2,387
Bonus Space: 377 sq. ft.
Bedrooms: 3
Bathrooms: 2½
Width: 69' - 6"
Depth: 68' - 11"
Foundation: Slab, Crawlspace

SEARCH ONLINE @ EPLANS.COM

FIRST FLOOR

ALTERNATE LAYOUT

This three-bedroom home brings the past to life with Tuscan columns, dormers, and fanlight windows. The entrance is flanked by the dining room and study. The great room boasts cathedral ceilings and a fireplace. The spacious kitchen adjoins a breakfast nook and accesses the rear covered veranda. The master bedroom enjoys a sitting area, access to the covered veranda, and a spacious bathroom. This home is complete with two family bedrooms.

Reminiscent of the grand homes of the Old South, this elegantly

appointed home is a beauty inside and out. A centerpiece stair rises gracefully from the two-story grand foyer and features balcony overlooks to the foyer and living room. The kitchen, breakfast room, and family room provide open space for the gathering of family and friends. The beam-ceilinged study and the dining room flank the grand foyer and each includes a fireplace. The master bedroom features a cozy sitting area and a luxury master bath with His and Hers vanities and walk-in closets. Three large bedrooms and a game room complete the second floor. A large expandable area is available at the top of the rear stair.

plan# HPK0700033

Style: Southern Colonial
First Floor: 3,170 sq. ft.
Second Floor: 1,914 sq. ft.
Total: 5,084 sq. ft.
Bonus Space: 445 sq. ft.
Bedrooms: 4
Bathrooms: 3½
Width: 100' - 10"
Depth: 65' - 5"
Foundation: Crawlspace

SEARCH ONLINE @ EPLANS.COM

FIRST FLOOR

SECOND FLOOR

ORDER BLUEPRINTS 24 HOURS, 7 DAYS A WEEK, AT 1-800-521-6797

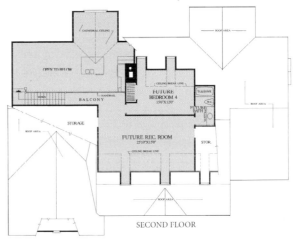

SECOND FLOOR

plan # HPK0700034

Style: Farmhouse
Square Footage: 2,777
Bonus Space: 424 sq. ft.
Bedrooms: 3
Bathrooms: 2½
Width: 75' - 6"
Depth: 60' - 2"
Foundation: Crawlspace,
Unfinished Basement

SEARCH ONLINE @ EPLANS.COM

This country cottage was designed for casual family living. The master suite is conveniently placed near the family bedrooms—perfect for young children. The living room has an attention-getting fireplace and built-in book cases. The gourmet kitchen is accented by a sloped ceiling, and the bumped-out breakfast area charms with a cathedral ceiling. Don't miss the family/sunroom, bathed in light year-round. An optional fourth bedroom and full bath, as well as future space, are available as your family grows.

FIRST FLOOR

OPTIONAL LAYOUT

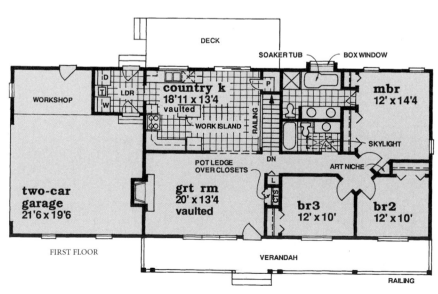

DECK

SOAKER TUB   BOX WINDOW

WORKSHOP

D
T
W   LDR

country k
18'11 x 13'4
vaulted

WORK ISLAND

RAILING

mbr
12' x 14'4

P

SKYLIGHT

POT LEDGE
OVER CLOSETS

DN

ART NICHE

two-car
garage
21'6 x 19'6

grt rm
20' x 13'4
vaulted

L
CSS

br3
12' x 10'

br2
12' x 10'

FIRST FLOOR

VERANDAH

RAILING

plan# HPK0700035

Style: Ranch
Square Footage: 1,408
Bedrooms: 3
Bathrooms: 2
Width: 70' - 0"
Depth: 34' - 0"
Foundation: Unfinished Basement,
Crawlspace

SEARCH ONLINE @ EPLANS.COM

Vaulted ceilings lend a sense of spaciousness to this three-bedroom home. A bright country kitchen boasts an abundance of counter space and cupboards. The front entry is sheltered by a broad veranda. A box-bay window and a spa-style tub highlight the master bedroom. The two-car garage provides a workshop area.

ON THE FARM

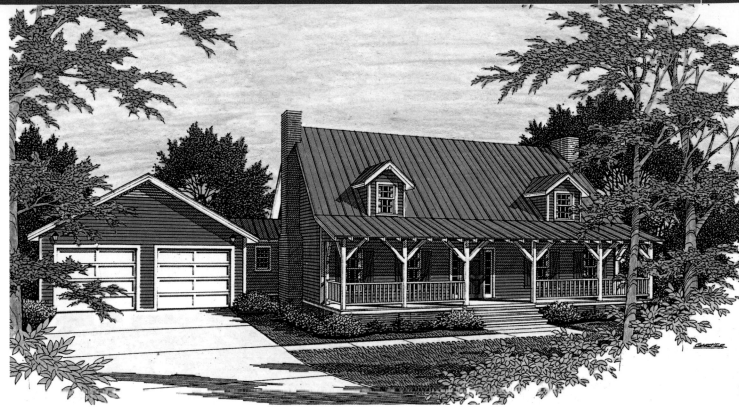

plan # HPK0700036

Style: Ranch
First Floor: 1,501 sq. ft.
Second Floor: 631 sq. ft.
Total: 2,132 sq. ft.
Bedrooms: 3
Bathrooms: 2½
Width: 76' 0"
Depth: 48' - 4"
Foundation: Slab, Unfinished Basement, Crawlspace

SEARCH ONLINE @ EPLANS.COM

This home reveals its rustic charm with a metal roof, dormers, and exposed-column rafters. The full-length porch is an invitation to comfortable living inside. The great room shares a fireplace with the spacious dining room that offers rear-porch access. The kitchen is this home's focus, with plenty of counter and cabinet space, a window sink, and an open layout.

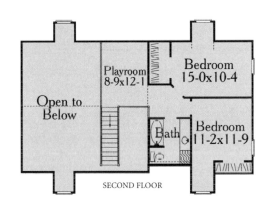

SECOND FLOOR

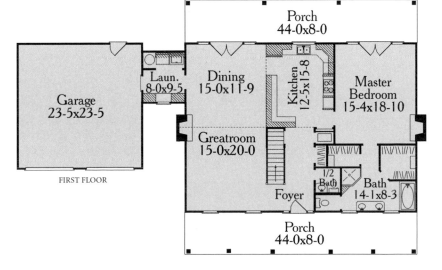

FIRST FLOOR

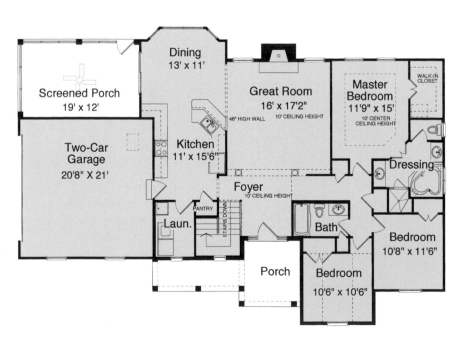

plan# HPK0700037

Style: Farmhouse
Square Footage: 1,611
Bedrooms: 3
Bathrooms: 2
Width: 66' - 4"
Depth: 43' - 10"
Foundation: Unfinished Basement

SEARCH ONLINE @ EPLANS.COM

A stone-and-siding exterior easily combines with the front covered porch on this three-bedroom ranch home. Inside, columns define the great room, which holds a warming fireplace framed by windows. The master bedroom enjoys a walk-in closet and a luxurious bath including a separate shower and a whirlpool tub. Two family bedrooms share a full bath and views of the front yard. Note the two-car side-access garage—perfect for a corner lot.

plan# HPK0700038

Style: Traditional
Square Footage: 1,594
Bedrooms: 3
Bathrooms: 2
Width: 52' - 8"
Depth: 55' - 5"
Foundation: Unfinished Basement

SEARCH ONLINE @ EPLANS.COM

Robin's Nest is a traditional western ranch home. The large island in the kitchen brings definition to the space, while angled windows decorate the eating area. Split bedrooms allow privacy for the master bedroom, which offers a private bath and laundry room access. Modify one of the family bedrooms into a library to create an exciting option.

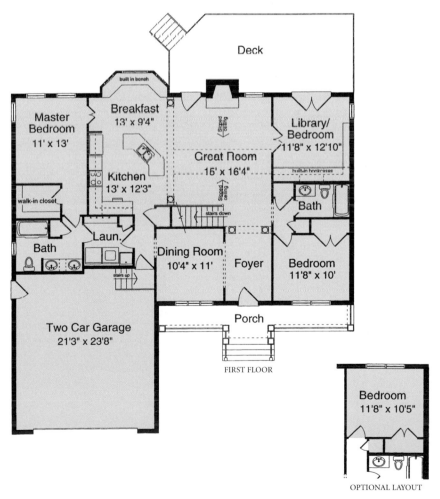

Deck

Master Bedroom
11' x 13'

Breakfast
13' x 9'4"

walk-in closet

Kitchen
13' x 12'3"

Great Room
15' x 16'4"

Library/Bedroom
11'8" x 12'10"

built-in bookcases

Bath

Laun.

Bath

stairs down

Bath

Dining Room
10'4" x 11'

Foyer

Bedroom
11'8" x 10'

stairs up

Two Car Garage
21'3" x 23'8"

Porch

FIRST FLOOR

Bedroom
11'8" x 10'5"

OPTIONAL LAYOUT

A wraparound porch and steep roofline, punctuated by small dormers, mark this farmhouse-style ranch home. The inviting foyer leads past a dining room with an enchanting stepped ceiling to the great room, which also enjoys an 11-foot-high ceiling. The delightful master suite includes a tray ceiling, a beautiful bay-window sitting area, two walk-in closets, and a lovely compartmented private bath with a whirlpool tub. Access to the master suite is very private and separated from the two front bedrooms. The high roofline provides for a huge bonus area.

plan# HPK0700039

Style: Farmhouse
Square Footage: 1,793
Bonus Space: 779 sq. ft.
Bedrooms: 3
Bathrooms: 2
Width: 69' - 10"
Depth: 51' - 8"
Foundation: Unfinished Basement, Slab, Crawlspace

SEARCH ONLINE @ EPLANS.COM

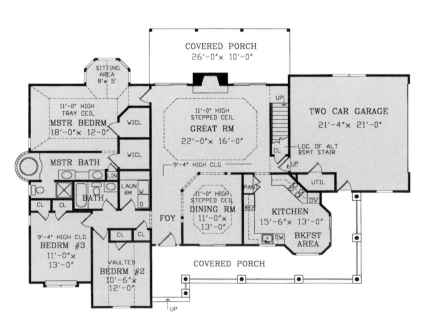

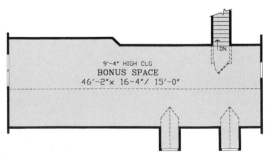

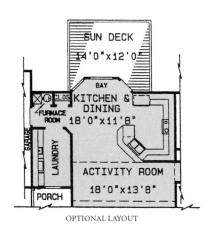

plan# HPK0700040

Style: Farmhouse
Square Footage: 1,352
Bedrooms: 3
Bathrooms: 2
Width: 71' - 6"
Depth: 36' - 0"
Foundation: Slab, Crawlspace,
Unfinished Walkout Basement

SEARCH ONLINE @ EPLANS.COM

The front covered porch that wraps around two sides of the house and the rear sundeck expand the living space of this modest one-story home. A lavish master suite with all the amenities you've dreamed about and two bedrooms that share a bath will make your family relaxed and comfortable. The kitchen, with a sweeping curved counter, is open to the dining areas and the living room. This not only enhances the feeling of open space, but makes serving both formal and informal meals a joy. A delightful breakfast bay that looks out over the sundeck will make the first morning cup of coffee something to remember. The well-equipped laundry is nestled between the kitchen and garage.

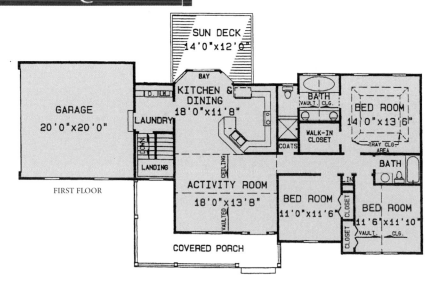

FIRST FLOOR

OPTIONAL LAYOUT

A simplified country facade suits the easy layout of this plan. Formal rooms flank the foyer, and the family room, kitchen, and breakfast nook will be the hub of casual living with their shared three-way fireplace. The master suite is secluded to the right, with an elegant bath and huge walk-in closet; the family bedrooms have their own space on the left.

plan# HPK0700041

Style: Farmhouse
Square Footage: 2,126
Bedrooms: 3
Bathrooms: 2
Width: 66' - 0"
Depth: 54' - 0"

SEARCH ONLINE @ EPLANS.COM

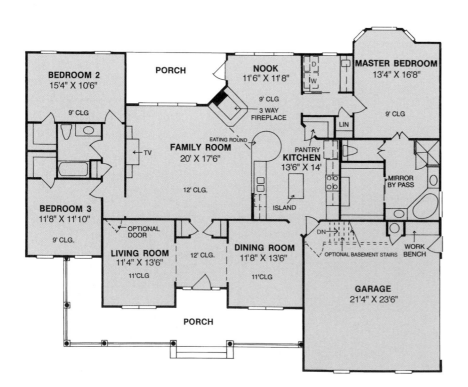

RUSTIC CABINS

Acountry home can be a great escape from the pressures of everyday life, whether it's a simple vacation retreat or a year-round home that's just far enough away from the cares of the office. Some of the best of these getaway homes are cabins, places where the architecture suggests seclusion but you can still find all the comforts of home.

Craftsman and bungalow styles abound among cabins, architectural genres that stress attention to detail and fine woodworking. Beautiful windows and prominent porches are other characteristics, both of which fit well in country homes. Large windows provide panoramic views and porches allow homeowners to take full advantage of lazy days.

These homes aren't ostentatious, but reflect fine craftsmanship. They fit into a rising demand among homeowners for quality over quantity, in a sense—the desire to not necessarily live in a larger home, but to enjoy a better home in a smaller space.

With intelligent floor plans and creative storage solutions, these designs might not strike you as overwhelming in size, but they could offer all that you and your family want in a new home. ■

With more than 3,800 square feet, Design HPK0700051 offers ample space, but with Craftsman detailing that preserves its rustic feel. Find more details on page 61.

This fine bungalow will be the envy of any neighborhood. The great room is enhanced by a beam ceiling, a through-fireplace, and French doors to the rear terrace. The U-shaped kitchen features a cooktop island. The master suite features a walk-in closet, a separate shower, and access to the terrace. Two secondary bedrooms share a full bath.

plan# HPK0700042

Style: Bungalow
Square Footage: 2,489
Bedrooms: 3
Bathrooms: 2½
Width: 68' - 3"
Depth: 62' - 0"
Foundation: Finished
Walkout Basement

SEARCH ONLINE @ EPLANS.COM

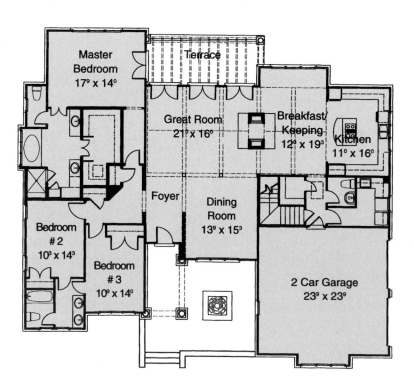

REAR EXTERIOR

plan# HPK0700043

Style: Craftsman
Main Level: 2,922 sq. ft.
Lower Level: 3,027 sq. ft.
Total: 5,949 sq. ft.
Bedrooms: 4
Bathrooms: 4½ + ½
Width: 98' 0"
Depth: 76' 0"
Foundation: Finished
Walkout Basement

SEARCH ONLINE @ EPLANS.COM

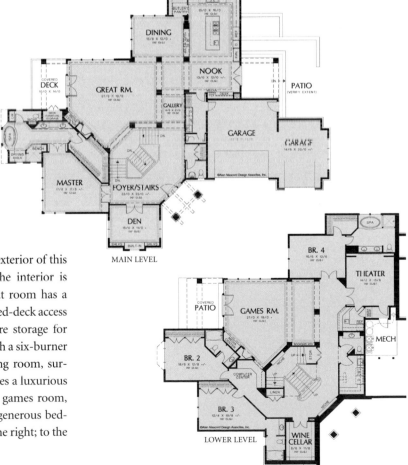

MAIN LEVEL

LOWER LEVEL

Looks can be deceiving! Although the exterior of this home appears as rustic as a mountain cabin, the interior is nothing but lavish. From a grand foyer, the great room has a warming fireplace and built-in media center. Covered-deck access is perfect year-round, with built-in deck furniture storage for those colder months. The kitchen is marvelous, with a six-burner cooktop island and a butler's pantry to the dining room, surrounded by glass. The inspiring master suite relishes a luxurious spa bath and tons of natural light. Downstairs, a games room, wine cellar, and theater are special touches. Two generous bedrooms share a full bath and a computer center to the right; to the left, Bedroom 4 enjoys a private spa bath.

This rustic stone and siding exterior with Craftsman influences includes a multitude of windows flooding the interior with natural light. The foyer opens to the great room, which is complete with three sets of French doors and a two-sided fireplace. The master suite offers an expansive private bath, two large walk-in closets, a bay window, and a tray ceiling. The dining room, kitchen, and utility room make an efficient trio.

plan# HPK0700044

Style: Bungalow
First Floor: 1,798 sq. ft.
Second Floor: 900 sq. ft.
Total: 2,698 sq. ft.
Bedrooms: 3
Bathrooms: 3
Width: 54' - 0"
Depth: 57' - 0"
Foundation: Crawlspace

SEARCH ONLINE @ EPLANS.COM

FIRST FLOOR

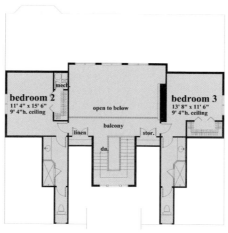

SECOND FLOOR

ORDER BLUEPRINTS 24 HOURS, 7 DAYS A WEEK, AT 1-800-521-6797

plan# HPK0700045

Style: Bungalow
First Floor: 2,391 sq. ft.
Second Floor: 1,539 sq. ft.
Total: 3,930 sq. ft.
Bedrooms: 3
Bathrooms: 4½
Width: 71' 0"
Depth: 69' 0"
Foundation: Island Basement

SEARCH ONLINE @ EPLANS.COM

Climate is a key component of any mountain retreat, and outdoor living is an integral part of its design. This superior cabin features open and covered porches. A mix of matchstick details and rugged stone set off this lodge-house facade, concealing a well-defined interior. Windows line the breakfast bay and brighten the kitchen, which features a center cooktop island. A door leads out to a covered porch with a summer kitchen. The upper level features a secluded master suite with a spacious bath beginning with a double walk-in closet and ending with a garden view of the porch. A two-sided fireplace extends warmth to the whirlpool spa-style tub.

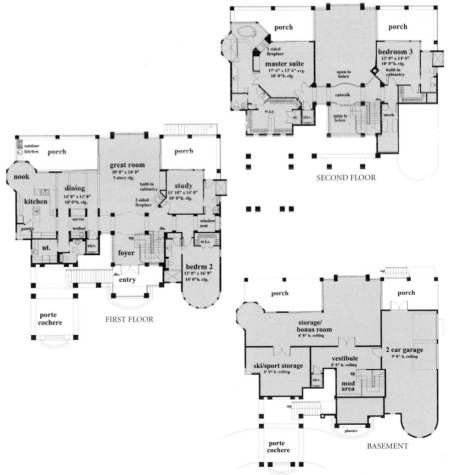

SECOND FLOOR

FIRST FLOOR

BASEMENT

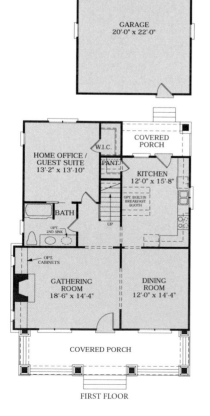

GARAGE
20'-0" x 22'-0"

COVERED
PORCH

W.I.C.

HOME OFFICE /
GUEST SUITE
13'-2" x 13'-10"

PANT.

KITCHEN
12'-0" x 15'-8"

OPT. BUILT-IN
BREAKFAST
BOOTH

BATH

OPT.
2ND SINK

UP

OPT.
CABINETS

GATHERING
ROOM
18'-6" x 14'-4"

DINING
ROOM
12'-0" x 14'-4"

COVERED PORCH

FIRST FLOOR

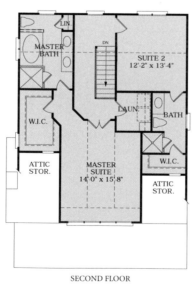

LIN

MASTER
BATH

DN

SUITE 2
12'-2" x 13'-4"

W.I.C.

LAUN

BATH

ATTIC
STOR.

MASTER
SUITE
14'-0" x 15'-8"

W.I.C.

ATTIC
STOR.

SECOND FLOOR

plan # HPK0700046

Style: Craftsman
First Floor: 1,060 sq. ft.
Second Floor: 914 sq. ft.
Total: 1,974 sq. ft.
Bedrooms: 3
Bathrooms: 3
Width: 32' - 0"
Depth: 35' - 0"
Foundation: Crawlspace

SEARCH ONLINE @ EPLANS.COM

This charming Craftsman design offers a second-story master bedroom with four windows under the gabled dormer. The covered front porch displays column and pier supports. The gathering room opens to the dining room on the right where the adjoining kitchen offers enough space for an optional breakfast booth. A home office/guest suite is found in the rear. The second floor holds the lavish master suite and a second bedroom with its own private bath.

plan # HPK0700047

Style: Bungalow
First Floor: 1,371 sq. ft.
Second Floor: 916 sq. ft.
Total: 2,287 sq. ft.
Bedrooms: 3
Bathrooms: 2½
Width: 43' - 0"
Depth: 69' - 0"
Foundation: Crawlspace

SEARCH ONLINE @ EPLANS.COM

Step up to this magnificent country farmhouse with a stunning wraparound porch and transom. To the left of the foyer is the den, featuring French doors and a passageway to the family room. The kitchen is complete with a cooktop island, built-in desk, and breakfast nook. Upstairs, the master bedroom presents a lavish private bath with a dual-sink vanity, corner whirlpool tub, separate shower, and vast walk-in closet.

SECOND FLOOR

FIRST FLOOR

SECOND FLOOR

REAR EXTERIOR

plan# HPK0700048

Style: Bungalow
First Floor: 1,143 sq. ft.
Second Floor: 651 sq. ft.
Total: 1,794 sq. ft.
Bonus Space: 651 sq. ft.
Bedrooms: 2
Bathrooms: 2½
Width: 32' - 0"
Depth: 57' - 0"
Foundation: Unfinished
Walkout Basement

SEARCH ONLINE @ EPLANS.COM

This traditional country cabin is a vacationer's dream. An elegant entryway extends into the foyer where the two-story great room visually expands the lofty interior. This room provides a warming fireplace and offers built-in cabinetry. The dining room opens through double doors to the veranda on the left side on the plan. Upstairs, a vaulted ceiling enhances the master suite.

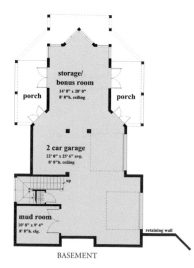

BASEMENT

FIRST FLOOR

plan # HPK0700049

Style: Bungalow
First Floor: 1,824 sq. ft.
Second Floor: 842 sq. ft.
Total: 2,666 sq. ft.
Bonus Space: 267 sq. ft.
Bedrooms: 3
Bathrooms: 3½
Width: 59' 0"
Depth: 53' - 6"
Foundation: Crawlspace

SEARCH ONLINE @ EPLANS.COM

SECOND FLOOR

Horizontal siding, double-hung windows,

and European gables lend a special charm to this contemporary home. The formal dining room opens from the foyer and offers a wet bar and a box-bay window. The great room features a fireplace and opens to a golf porch as well as a charming side porch. A well-lit kitchen contains a cooktop island counter and two pantries. The first-floor master suite has a tray ceiling, a box-bay window, and a deluxe bath with a garden tub and an angled shower. Both of the upper-level bedrooms privately access a full bath.

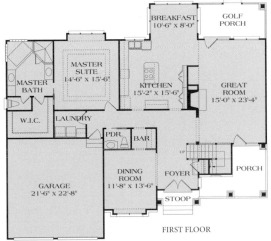

FIRST FLOOR

This impressive two-story Craftsman design features a modern layout filled with abundant rooms and amenities. A wide front porch welcomes you inside to an entry flanked on either side by formal living and dining rooms. Built-ins enhance the dining room, while the living room shares a see-through fireplace with the library/study. The island kitchen offers a utility room and food pantry nearby, and overlooks the breakfast and family rooms. The mudroom accesses the rear porch and sun room. The luxurious master suite contains a sitting area, His and Hers walk-in closets, a private bath, and an exercise room. At the rear, planters enhance the raised patio area. The second floor features three additional bedrooms. A study between Bedrooms 3 and 4 is perfect for the kids. A game room, sleep loft, and rear balcony complete this floor.

plan# HPK0700050

Style: Craftsman
First Floor: 3,253 sq. ft.
Second Floor: 1,747 sq. ft.
Total: 5,000 sq. ft.
Bedrooms: 5
Bathrooms: 5½
Width: 112' - 9"
Depth: 89' - 10"
Foundation: Crawlspace

SEARCH ONLINE @ EPLANS.COM

FIRST FLOOR

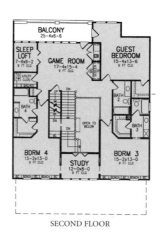

SECOND FLOOR

ORDER BLUEPRINTS 24 HOURS, 7 DAYS A WEEK, AT 1-800-521-6797

plan(#) HPK0700051

Design: HPK0700051
Style: Craftsman
First Floor: 2,120 sq. ft.
Second Floor: 1,520 sq. ft.
Third Floor: 183 sq. ft.
Total: 3,823 sq. ft.
Bedrooms: 5
Bathrooms: 4½ + ½
Width: 76' - 0"
Depth: 81' - 0"
Foundation: Finished Walkout Basement, Slab, Crawlspace

SEARCH ONLINE @ EPLANS.COM

The rustic chic of Craftsman details makes this an unusual example of estate architecture. But, extravagant floor planning leaves no doubt that luxury is what this home is about. The first floor has open spaces for living: a reading room and dining room flanking the foyer, a huge family room with built-ins and fireplace plus covered deck access, and an island kitchen and nook with built-in table. The first-floor master suite is graced with a beamed ceiling. Its attached bath is well appointed and spacious. On the second floor are four bedrooms and three baths. Third-floor attic space can be used for whatever suits you best. Don't miss the home theater that can be developed in the basement and home-office space over the garage.

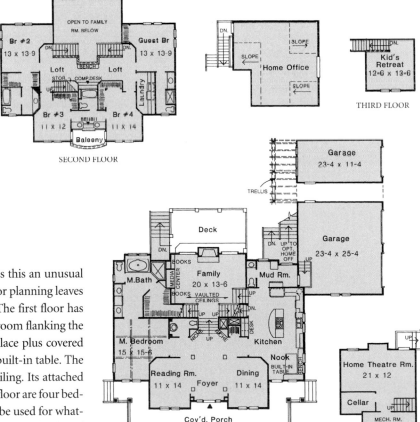

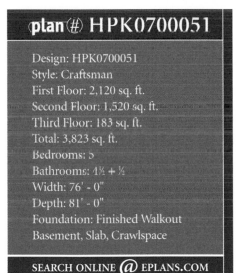

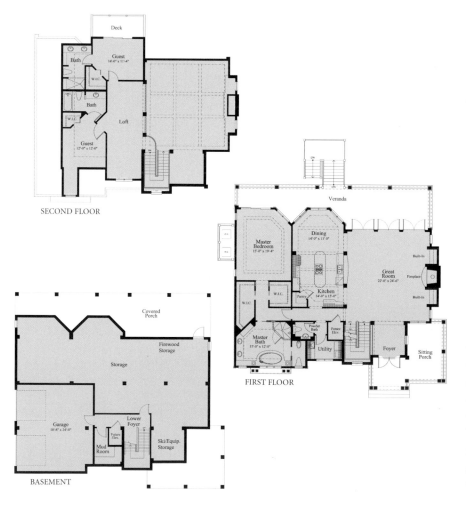

Deck

Guest
14'-0" x 13'-4"

Bath

W.I.C.

Bath

Loft

W.I.C.

Guest
12'-0" x 12'-0"

SECOND FLOOR

Veranda

Master
Bedroom
15'-0" x 19'-4"

Dining
14'-0" x 11'-0"

Kitchen
14'-0" x 15'-0"

Great
Room
22'-0" x 24'-6"

Fireplace

Built-In

Built-In

W.I.C.

Pantry

Master
Bath
15'-0" x 12'-0"

W.I.C.

Powder
Bath

Future Elev.

Utility

Foyer

Sitting
Porch

FIRST FLOOR

Covered
Porch

Firewood
Storage

Storage

Garage
19'-6" x 24'-0"

Future Elev.

Mud
Room

Lower
Foyer

Ski/Equip.
Storage

BASEMENT

plan # HPK0700052

Style: Bungalow
First Floor: 2,096 sq. ft.
Second Floor: 892 sq. ft.
Total: 2,988 sq. ft.
Bedrooms: 3
Bathrooms: 3½
Width: 56' - 0"
Depth: 54' - 0"
Foundation: Unfinished
Walkout Basement

SEARCH ONLINE @ EPLANS.COM

Siding and shingles give this

home a Craftsman look while columns and gables suggest a more traditional style. The foyer opens to a short flight of stairs that leads to the great room, which features a lovely coffered ceiling, a fireplace, built-ins, and French doors to the rear veranda. To the left, the open, island kitchen enjoys a pass-through to the great room and easy service to the dining bay. The secluded master suite has two walk-in closets, a luxurious bath, and veranda access. Upstairs, two family bedrooms enjoy their own full baths and share a loft area.

plan# HPK0700053

Style: Craftsman
First Floor: 1,322 sq. ft.
Second Floor: 1,262 sq. ft.
Total: 2,584 sq. ft.
Bedrooms: 4
Bathrooms: 3
Width: 48' - 0"
Depth: 50' - 0"
Foundation: Crawlspace,
Unfinished Walkout Basement, Slab

SEARCH ONLINE @ EPLANS.COM

SECOND FLOOR

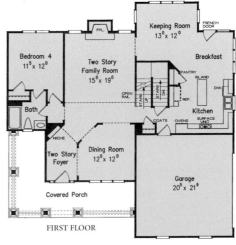

FIRST FLOOR

With Craftsman detail and traditional

charm, this four-bedroom home captures the comfort and style you've been searching for. From a wrapping porch, enter the two-story foyer with a decorative niche that displays special photos or treasures to all your guests. Continue to a beautiful family room, graced with a two-story ceiling and second-floor radius windows. The kitchen is open and spacious, leading to a breakfast area, hearth-warmed keeping room, and elegant dining room. A bedroom on this level also serves as an ideal den or home office. Upstairs, two secondary bedrooms share a full bath. The master suite is ready for relaxation with a sunny sitting room and soothing vaulted bath. A laundry room on this level makes wash day a breeze.

The horizontal siding of this facade evokes a sense of charm and comfort similar to a log cabin. The covered porch opens to a foyer, flanked by a study on the left and the dining room on the right. Beyond the foyer sits the living room, complete with a fireplace and double-door access to the large rear deck. To the right of the living room, a second fireplace in the family room warms the large country kitchen, and the nearby utility room and office. An island snack bar in the kitchen conveniently serves the family room. On the opposite side of the floor plan, the master suite offers a private entrance to the rear deck, His and Hers walk-in closets, a dual sink vanity, a compartmented toilet, a separate shower, and a garden tub. Upstairs, three family bedrooms, each with a walk-in closet, share two full baths.

plan # HPK0700054

Style: Cabin
First Floor: 2,589 sq. ft.
Second Floor: 981 sq. ft.
Total: 3,570 sq. ft.
Bedrooms: 4
Bathrooms: 3½
Width: 70' - 8"
Depth: 61' - 10"
Foundation: Crawlspace

SEARCH ONLINE @ EPLANS.COM

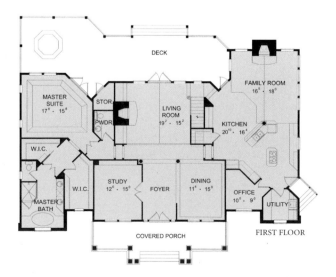

ORDER BLUEPRINTS 24 HOURS, 7 DAYS A WEEK, AT 1-800-521-6797

plan # HPK0700055

Style: Craftsman
Main Level: 2,172 sq. ft.
Lower Level: 1,813 sq. ft.
Total: 3,985 sq. ft.
Bedrooms: 4
Bathrooms: 3½
Width: 75' - 0"
Depth: 49' - 0"
Foundation: Finished
Walkout Basement

SEARCH ONLINE @ EPLANS.COM

With the Craftsman stylings of a mountain lodge, this rustic four-bedroom home is full of surprises. The foyer opens to the right to the great room, warmed by a stone hearth. A corner media center is convenient for entertaining. The dining room, with a furniture alcove, opens to the side terrace, inviting meals alfresco. An angled kitchen provides lots of room to move. The master suite is expansive, with French doors, a private bath, and spa tub. On the lower level, two bedrooms share a bath; a third enjoys a private suite. The games room includes a fireplace, media center, wet bar, and wine cellar. Don't miss the storage capacity and work area in the garage.

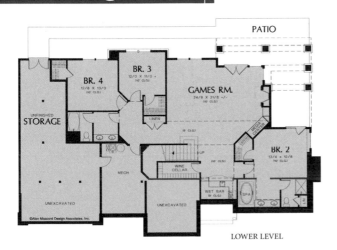

LOWER LEVEL

MAIN LEVEL

SECOND FLOOR

FIRST FLOOR

plan# HPK0700056

Style: Craftsman
First Floor: 1,761 sq. ft.
Second Floor: 577 sq. ft.
Total: 2,338 sq. ft.
Bonus Space: 305 sq. ft.
Bedrooms: 4
Bathrooms: 3
Width: 56' - 0"
Depth: 48' - 0"
Foundation: Crawlspace,
Unfinished Walkout Basement

SEARCH ONLINE @ EPLANS.COM

Craftsman-style pillars lend a country look to this Cape Cod-style home. An elegant entry opens to the vaulted family room, where a fireplace warms and bright windows illuminate. The kitchen is designed for the true chef, with step-saving orientation and a serving bar to the vaulted breakfast nook. A bedroom nearby is ideal for a home office or live-in help. The master suite is on the left, pampering with a vaulted bath and enormous walk-in closet. Two bedrooms upstairs share a full bath and an optional bonus room.

plan(#) HPK0700057

Style: Craftsman
First Floor: 2,782 sq. ft.
Second Floor: 1,027 sq. ft.
Total: 3,809 sq. ft.
Bedrooms: 4
Bathrooms: 4½
Width: 78' - 2"
Depth: 74' - 6"
Foundation: Finished
Walkout Basement

SEARCH ONLINE @ EPLANS.COM

Filled with specialty rooms and abundant amenities, this countryside house is the perfect dream home. Double doors open into an angled foyer, flanked by a music room and a formal great room warmed by a fireplace. The music room leads to the master wing of the home, which includes a spacious bath with a dressing area and double walk-in closet. The great room is the heart of the home—its central position allows access to the island kitchen, formal dining room, and library. Stairs behind the kitchen lead upstairs to a balcony, accessing three family bedrooms. The lower level features a billiard room, hobby room, media room, and future possibilities.

REAR EXTERIOR

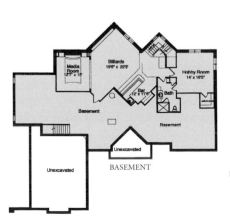

BASEMENT

FIRST FLOOR

SECOND FLOOR

SECOND FLOOR

FIRST FLOOR

Bedroom 3
13⁰ x 12⁴

W.i.c.

Optional
Bonus Room
14⁹ x 11⁹

W.i.c.

Family Room
Below

OPEN
RAIL

LINEN

OVERLOOK

STAIRS
DN

Bath

W.i.c.

Bedroom 2
12³ x 11⁶

TRAY CEILING

Master Suite
17⁰ x 13³

W.i.c.

LINEN

FRENCH
DOOR

PANTRY
DOOR

K.S.

Vaulted
M. Bath

SEAT
SHWR.

W.
D.

NICHE

FRENCH
DOOR

RADIUS
WINDOW

COATS

Breakfast

ISLAND

RANGE

Kitchen

DW

REF

PANT.

FPL

Vaulted
Family Room
16⁰ x 19²

Garage
19⁹ x 19⁹

Dining Room
14⁹ x 12⁰

STAIRS
DN

STAIRS
UP

OPEN RAIL

Foyer

Pdr.

Covered Porch

plan # HPK0700058

Style: Craftsman
First Floor: 1,561 sq. ft.
Second Floor: 578 sq. ft.
Total: 2,139 sq. ft.
Bonus Space: 238 sq. ft.
Bedrooms: 3
Bathrooms: 2½
Width: 50' - 0"
Depth: 56' - 6"
Foundation: Crawlspace,
Unfinished Walkout Basement

SEARCH ONLINE @ EPLANS.COM

Come home to this delightful bungalow, created with you in mind. From the covered front porch, the foyer opens to the dining room on the left and vaulted family room ahead. An elongated island in the well-planned kitchen makes meal preparation a joy. A sunny breakfast nook is perfect for casual pursuits. Tucked to the rear, the master suite enjoys ultimate privacy and a luxurious break from the world with a vaulted bath and garden tub. Secondary bedrooms share a full bath upstairs; a bonus room is ready to expand as your needs change.

© Stephen Fuller, Inc.

plan # HPK0700059

Style: Bungalow
First Floor: 1,924 sq. ft.
Second Floor: 1,097 sq. ft.
Total: 3,021 sq. ft.
Bonus Space: 352 sq. ft.
Bedrooms: 3
Bathrooms: 2½
Width: 68' - 3"
Depth: 53' - 0"
Foundation: Crawlspace

SEARCH ONLINE @ EPLANS.COM

This lovely Craftsman-style home invites enjoyment of
the outdoors with a front covered porch and a spacious rear terrace.
Inside, formal rooms flank the foyer and feature lovely amenities such
as French-door access to the front porch. A fireplace warms the family
room, which provides plenty of natural light and wide views through
three sets of glass doors. Additional bedrooms on the second floor
enjoy a balcony overlook to the family room.

SECOND FLOOR

FIRST FLOOR

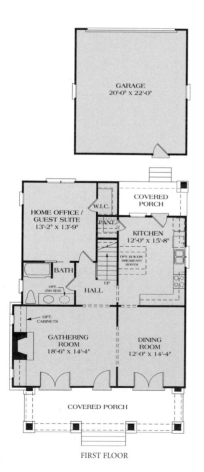

GARAGE
20'-0" x 22'-0"

HOME OFFICE /
GUEST SUITE
13'-2" x 13'-9"

W.I.C.

COVERED
PORCH

PANT.

KITCHEN
12'-0" x 15'-8"

OPT. BUILT-IN
BREAKFAST
BOOTH

BATH

OPT.
2ND SINK

HALL

UP

OPT.
CABINETS

GATHERING
ROOM
18'-6" x 14'-4"

DINING
ROOM
12'-0" x 14'-4"

COVERED PORCH

FIRST FLOOR

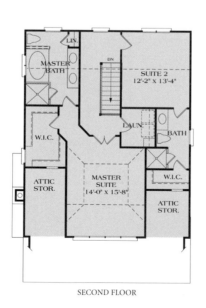

LIN.

MASTER
BATH

DN

SUITE 2
12'-2" x 13'-4"

W.I.C.

LAUN.

BATH

ATTIC
STOR.

MASTER
SUITE
14'-0" x 15'-8"

W.I.C.

ATTIC
STOR.

SECOND FLOOR

plan# HPK0700060

Style: Bungalow
First Floor: 1,061 sq. ft.
Second Floor: 914 sq. ft.
Total: 1,975 sq. ft.
Bedrooms: 3
Bathrooms: 3
Width: 32' - 0"
Depth: 45' - 0"
Foundation: Crawlspace

SEARCH ONLINE @ EPLANS.COM

A charming shape and amazing natural light mark this well-planned bungalow with comfort and personality. Enter from the covered front porch—two sets of French doors frame the main entrance. The gathering room is presented with a cozy fireplace and opens to the airy dining room. The large kitchen is designed to include a handy breakfast booth. At the rear, a home office (or guest suite) affords plenty of privacy. Upstairs, the master suite delights in an oversized shed dormer window and a vaulted spa bath. An additional bedroom suite completes the plan.

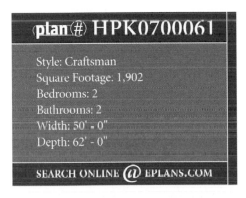

plan# HPK0700061

Style: Craftsman
Square Footage: 1,902
Bedrooms: 2
Bathrooms: 2
Width: 50' - 0"
Depth: 62' - 0"

SEARCH ONLINE @ EPLANS.COM

Columns decorate the covered porch and a dormer accents the rooftop of this classic bungalow home. The foyer leads into the great room, which is warmed by a fireplace. The breakfast room brightens the island kitchen. A sitting room is featured in the master suite, along with a spacious walk-in closet and pampering bath. French doors open into a third bedroom or den.

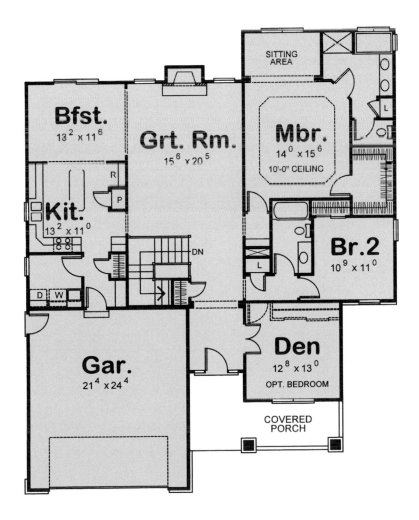

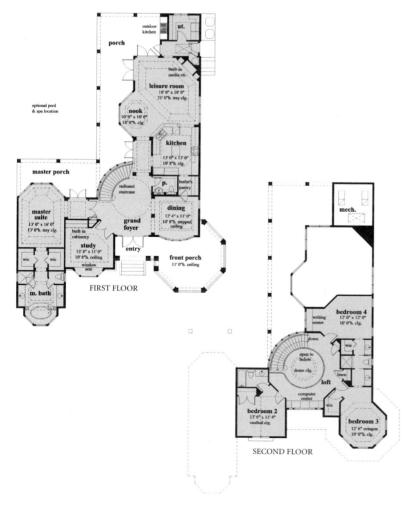

FIRST FLOOR

SECOND FLOOR

plan# HPK0700062

Style: Bungalow
First Floor: 2,083 sq. ft.
Second Floor: 1,013 sq. ft.
Total: 3,096 sq. ft.
Bedrooms: 4
Bathrooms: 3½
Width: 59' - 6"
Depth: 88' - 0"
Foundation: Slab

SEARCH ONLINE @ EPLANS.COM

This dream cabin captures the finest historic details in rooms furnished with comfort and style. A grand foyer features a radius staircase that decks out the entry hall and defines the wide-open interior. A formal dining room is served through a butler's pantry by a well-equipped kitchen. Casual space includes a leisure room that sports a corner fireplace, tray ceiling, and built-in media center. An outdoor kitchen makes it easy to enjoy life outside on the wraparound porch. The main-level master suite is suited with a spacious bedroom, two walk-in closets, and a lavish bath with separate vanities and a bumped-out whirlpool tub. Upstairs, two family bedrooms share a compartmented bath, and a guest suite boasts a roomy bath.

plan # HPK0700063

Style: Craftsman

First Floor: 2,665 sq. ft.

Second Floor: 1,081 sq. ft.

Total: 3,746 sq. ft.

Bedrooms: 4

Bathrooms: 3½

Width: 88' - 0"

Depth: 52' - 6"

Foundation: Unfinished
Walkout Basement

SEARCH ONLINE @ EPLANS.COM

This lovely plan steps into the future with an exterior mix of brick, stone and cedar siding. With a large front porch, the home appears as if it should be located in a quaint oceanfront community. Comfortable elegance coupled with modern-day amenities and nostalgic materials makes this home a great choice. The large great room and hearth room/breakfast area offer grand views to the rear yard, where a large deck complements outdoor activities.

SECOND FLOOR

plan# HPK0700064

Style: Craftsman
First Floor: 1,799 sq. ft.
Second Floor: 709 sq. ft.
Total: 2,508 sq. ft.
Bonus Space: 384 sq. ft.
Bedrooms: 3
Bathrooms: 2½
Width: 77' - 4"
Depth: 41' - 4"
Foundation: Unfinished
Walkout Basement

SEARCH ONLINE @ EPLANS.COM

FIRST FLOOR

An oversized dormer above the entryway and a steep, side-gabled roof bring an interesting front perspective to this Craftsman-style vacation home. Inside, a wood-burning fireplace warms the family room, overlooked by the second-floor walkway. To the left, the master suite is attended by a large walk-in closet and double vanities in the bathroom. Owners will also appreciate the private access to the deck. The full-sized garage at the right of the plan features a bonus room on the upper floor.

ORDER BLUEPRINTS 24 HOURS, 7 DAYS A WEEK, AT 1-800-521-6797

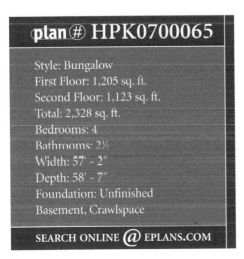

plan # HPK0700065

Style: Bungalow
First Floor: 1,205 sq. ft.
Second Floor: 1,123 sq. ft.
Total: 2,328 sq. ft.
Bedrooms: 4
Bathrooms: 2½
Width: 57' - 2"
Depth: 58' - 7"
Foundation: Unfinished Basement, Crawlspace

SEARCH ONLINE @ EPLANS.COM

FIRST FLOOR

SECOND FLOOR

With Craftsman details and modern amenities, this design offers an attractive layout. The long foyer opens to the dining and living rooms, which enjoy a flowing space. The family room features a corner fireplace and access to the rear grounds. The breakfast nook sports French doors which liven-up the nearby island kitchen with natural light. Upstairs, the master bedroom luxuriates with a spa tub, dual vanities, shower, and an oversized walk-in closet.

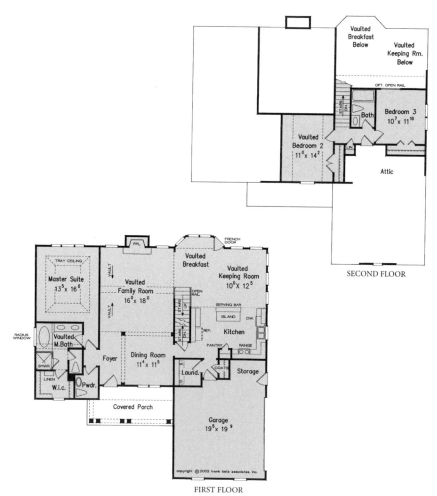

Vaulted
Breakfast
Below

Vaulted
Keeping Rm.
Below

OPT. OPEN RAIL

Bath

Bedroom 3
10⁷ x 11¹⁰

STAIRS DN

Vaulted
Bedroom 2
11⁰ x 14²

LIN

Attic

SECOND FLOOR

TRAY CEILING

Master Suite
13⁵ x 16⁰

Vaulted
Family Room
16⁹ x 18⁰

VAULT

VAULT

Vaulted
Breakfast

FRENCH
DOOR

PPL.

Vaulted
Keeping Room
10⁰ x 12⁵

SERVING BAR

ISLAND

DW.

OPEN
RAIL

REF.

Kitchen

RADIUS
WINDOW

Vaulted
M.Bath

SHWR

Foyer

Dining Room
11⁴ x 11⁵

PANTRY

RANGE

STAIRS UP

LINEN

W.i.c.

Pwdr.

COATS

Laund.

W.
D.

Storage

Covered Porch

Garage
19⁵ x 19⁹

copyright © 2002 frank betz associates, inc.

FIRST FLOOR

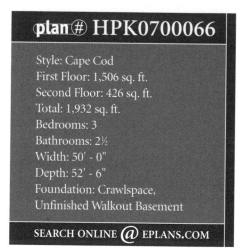

plan# HPK0700066

Style: Cape Cod
First Floor: 1,506 sq. ft.
Second Floor: 426 sq. ft.
Total: 1,932 sq. ft.
Bedrooms: 3
Bathrooms: 2½
Width: 50' - 0"
Depth: 52' - 6"
Foundation: Crawlspace,
Unfinished Walkout Basement

SEARCH ONLINE @ EPLANS.COM

A Craftsman cottage with careful detailing, this sweet country home is sure to please. From the covered porch, the foyer reveals an open floor plan. The dining room, defined by columns, leads into the vaulted family room. Here, a fireplace framed by windows makes this comfortable space feel cozy. The vaulted breakfast and keeping rooms are bathed in light; easy access to the gourmet kitchen includes a serving-bar island. The master suite features a vaulted spa bath with a radius window and a garden tub. Upstairs, two bedrooms share a full bath.

plan # HPK0700067

Style: Bungalow
Square Footage: 1,275
Bedrooms: 3
Bathrooms: 2
Width: 40' - 0"
Depth: 58' - 0"
Foundation: Crawlspace

SEARCH ONLINE @ EPLANS.COM

This handsome bungalow is very practical, yet comfortable, for the active family. The kitchen, dining area, and living room are organized for great efficiency in preparing and serving meals and snacks and for warm social and family gatherings. The dining nook opens to the rear patio through a sliding glass door, and the living room looks through a bay window onto the front covered porch. Columns separate the kitchen and dining area from the living room, which features a vaulted ceiling and fireplace. A vaulted ceiling soars above the master bedchamber; the adjoining private bath enjoys a dual-sink vanity and a combined shower/tub. Two other bedrooms share a bath.

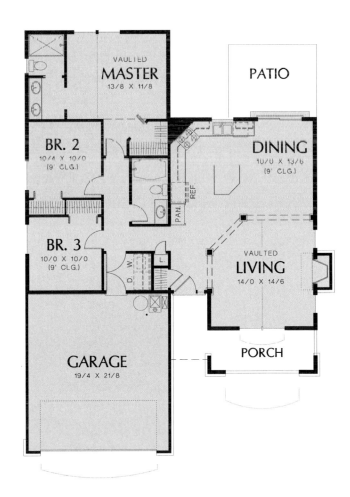

SECOND FLOOR

FIRST FLOOR

plan# HPK0700068

Style: Cabin
First Floor: 2,589 sq. ft.
Second Floor: 981 sq. ft.
Total: 3,570 sq. ft.
Bedrooms: 4
Bathrooms: 3½
Width: 70' - 8"
Depth: 61' - 10"
Foundation: Crawlspace

SEARCH ONLINE @ EPLANS.COM

Decidedly rustic with exposed truss work and wood exterior, this home has natural appeal. A spacious floor plan maximizes open space with formal rooms flanking the foyer and giving way to a comfortable living room with fireplace and rear deck access. A casual room grouping that includes an island kitchen, family room, office, eating area, and utility room, will be the hub of family activity. Let the master suite entice you to relax in privacy and enjoy a hot bath or a great view of the rear landscape and deck. Three family bedrooms are outfitted with walk-in closets and access to two full baths.

plan # HPK0700069

Style: Cabin
Square Footage: 2,019
Bedrooms: 3
Bathrooms: 2
Width: 56' - 0"
Depth: 56' - 3"
Foundation: Crawlspace

SEARCH ONLINE @ EPLANS.COM

REAR EXTERIOR

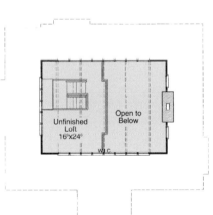

This design takes inspiration from the casual fishing cabins of the Pacific Northwest and interprets it for modern livability. It offers three options for a main entrance. One door opens to a mud porch, while two French doors on the side porch open into a dining room with bay-window seating. Another porch entrance opens directly into the great room. The secluded master bedroom features a bath with a claw-foot tub and twin pedestal sinks. Two more bedrooms share a bath.

Brackets and balustrades on front and rear covered porches spell old-fashioned country charm on this rustic retreat. In cooler weather, the raised-hearth fireplace will make the great room a cozy place to gather. Two family bedrooms and a full bath complete the main level. Upstairs, a master bedroom with a sloped ceiling offers a window seat and a complete bath. The adjacent loft/study overlooks the great room.

plan# HPK0700070

Style: Cabin **L D**
First Floor: 1,093 sq. ft.
Second Floor: 580 sq. ft.
Total: 1,673 sq. ft.
Bedrooms: 3
Bathrooms: 2
Width: 36' - 0"
Depth: 52' - 0"
Foundation: Crawlspace

SEARCH ONLINE @ EPLANS.COM

QUOTE ONE®

FIRST FLOOR

SECOND FLOOR

Welcome home to a petite cottage that is economical to build and has plenty to offer. Enter from the covered porch to a family room with great views and a warming fireplace. The sunny dining area is adjacent and can be as formal or casual as you wish. The kitchen is planned for efficiency and hosts a serving bar and rear-porch access, perfect for outdoor dining. Three family bedrooms include a master suite with a private bath and two additional bedrooms that share a full bath.

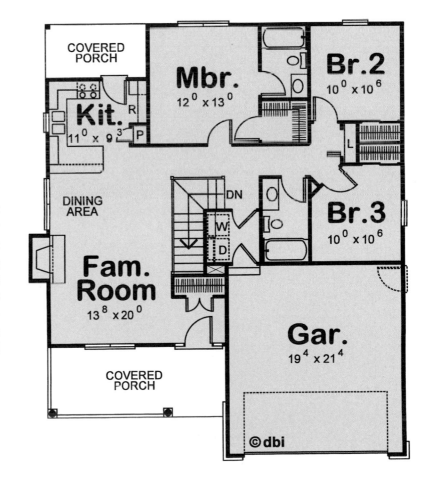

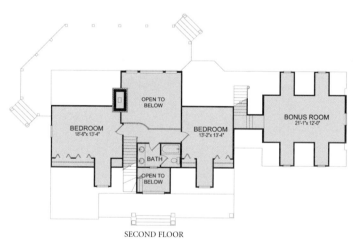

SECOND FLOOR

BEDROOM
18'-6"x 13'-4"

OPEN TO BELOW

BEDROOM
13'-2"x 13'-4"

BONUS ROOM
21'-1"x 12'-0"

BATH

OPEN TO BELOW

plan # HPK0700072

Style: Craftsman
First Floor: 1,799 sq. ft.
Second Floor: 709 sq. ft.
Total: 2,508 sq. ft.
Bonus Space: 384 sq. ft.
Bedrooms: 3
Bathrooms: 2½
Width: 77' - 4"
Depth: 41' - 4"
Foundation: Unfinished
Walkout Basement

SEARCH ONLINE @ EPLANS.COM

DECK

MASTER
15'-8"x 19'-3"

FAMILY
17'-8"x 19'-1"

NOOK
11'-1"x 9'-5"

GARAGE
21'-1"x 23'-9"

KITCHEN
13'-5"x 15'-6"

UTIL

BATH

W.I.C.

FOYER

DINING
15'-10"x 11'-6"

BATH

ENTRY

FIRST FLOOR

Beautiful wood details frame the windows

and front entry of this appealing design. The foyer introduces the dining room to the right and the family room at the rear. An open island kitchen and adjoining nook create a welcoming and versitile space with the family room. Privacy and comfort can be found in the first-floor master suite. Upstairs, two family bedrooms share a full hall bath. A bonus room sits above the garage and is accessible from the garage entry.

COZY COTTAGES

Cottages, even those in suburban areas, capture a distinctly country flavor. They are gorgeous in their simplicity, and feature a timeless look that's as attractive in new homes now as it was two centuries ago.

As lot sizes shrink, homeowners search for ways to enjoy the most possible living space on a smaller footprint. Quaint but well-thought-out, cottages can be the perfect solution—and they come equipped with a healthy dose of country charm.

A big part of both of these ideas—making the most of limited space and capturing the country spirit—can be found in the great rooms that have gained popularity in today's cottages. Here the whole family can gather around the hearth, creating a sense of togetherness even if everyone is doing their own thing. There's room here for watching TV, reading the paper, writing a homework assignment, and eating a quick snack.

Just steps from most great rooms, the country kitchen has always been at the heart of the best cottages. Its beauty and practicality make the country kitchen a gathering place for the family, with the space to prepare large meals and a decor that balances modern appliances with country-styled accessories.∎

A bright red roof and stark white siding lend a comfortable charm to Design HPK0700051. Turn to page 107 for more details.

Compact yet comfortable, this country cottage offers many appealing ameni-ties. From a covered front porch that invites relaxed living, the entrance opens to the living room with access to the dining room and snack bar. Two bedrooms are secluded to the right of the plan; the kitchen, bathroom, and laundry facilities are located on the left side. A second porch off the kitchen provides room for more casual dining and quiet moments.

plan # HPK0700073

Style: Country Cottage
Square Footage: 920
Bedrooms: 2
Bathrooms: 1
Width: 38' - 0"
Depth: 28' - 0"
Foundation: Unfinished Basement

SEARCH ONLINE @ EPLANS.COM

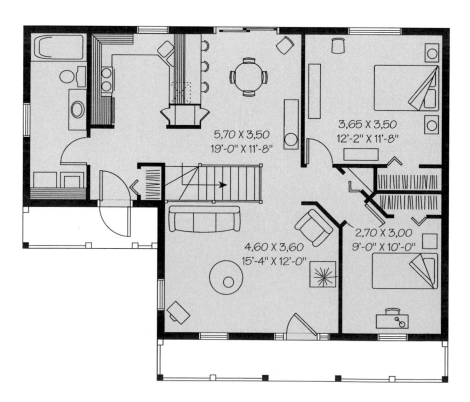

5,70 X 3,50
19'-0" X 11'-8"

3,65 X 3,50
12'-2" X 11'-8"

4,60 X 3,60
15'-4" X 12'-0"

2,70 X 3,00
9'-0" X 10'-0"

ORDER BLUEPRINTS 24 HOURS, 7 DAYS A WEEK, AT 1-800-521-6797

plan # HPK0700074

Style: Country Cottage
Square Footage: 2,151
Bonus Space: 814 sq. ft.
Bedrooms: 3
Bathrooms: 2
Width: 61' - 0"
Depth: 55' - 8"
Foundation: Crawlspace, Unfinished Basement

SEARCH ONLINE @ EPLANS.COM

Country flavor is well established on this fine three-bedroom home. The covered front porch welcomes friends and family alike to the foyer, where the formal dining room opens off to the left. The vaulted ceiling in the great room enhances the warmth of the fireplace and wall of windows. An efficient kitchen works well with the bayed breakfast area. The secluded master suite offers a walk-in closet and a lavish bath; on the other side of the home, two family bedrooms share a full bath. Upstairs, an optional fourth bedroom is available for guests or in-laws and provides access to a large recreation room.

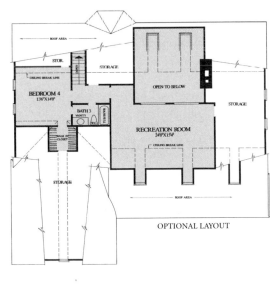

OPTIONAL LAYOUT

FIRST FLOOR

The expansive covered front porch offers protection from the heat of the summer. Graceful columns define the formal dining room and living room where a tray ceiling follows the contours created by the corner fireplace. The left side of the home holds the bedrooms and baths while the right side keeps the kitchen, breakfast nook and the utility room that offers access to the two-car garage.

plan# HPK0700075

Style: Country Cottage
Square Footage: 1,500
Bedrooms: 3
Bathrooms: 2
Width: 64' - 0"
Depth: 45' - 0"
Foundation: Slab

SEARCH ONLINE @ EPLANS.COM

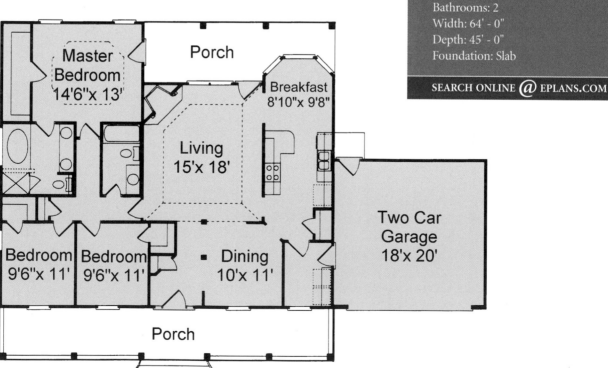

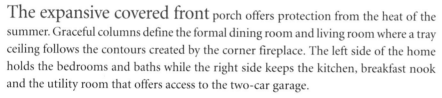

Master Bedroom 14'6"x 13'

Porch

Breakfast 8'10"x 9'8"

Living 15'x 18'

Bedroom 9'6"x 11'

Bedroom 9'6"x 11'

Dining 10'x 11'

Two Car Garage 18'x 20'

Porch

plan # HPK0700076

Style: Country Cottage
First Floor: 2,142 sq. ft.
Second Floor: 960 sq. ft.
Total: 3,102 sq. ft.
Bonus Space: 327 sq. ft.
Bedrooms: 4
Bathrooms: 3½
Width: 75' - 8"
Depth: 53' - 0"
Foundation: Crawlspace

SEARCH ONLINE @ EPLANS.COM

SECOND FLOOR

FIRST FLOOR

Imagine driving up to this cottage beauty at the
end of a long week. The long wraparound porch, hipped
rooflines, and shuttered windows will transport you. Inside,
the foyer is flanked by a living room on the left and a formal
dining room on the right. Across the gallery hall, the hearth-
warmed family room will surely become the hub of the home.
To the right, the spacious kitchen boasts a worktop island
counter, ample pantry space, and a breakfast area. A short
hallway opens to the utility room and the two-car garage. The
master suite takes up the entire left wing of the home, enjoying
an elegant private bath and a walk-in closet that goes on and
on. Upstairs, three more bedrooms reside, sharing two full
baths. Expandable future space awaits on the right.

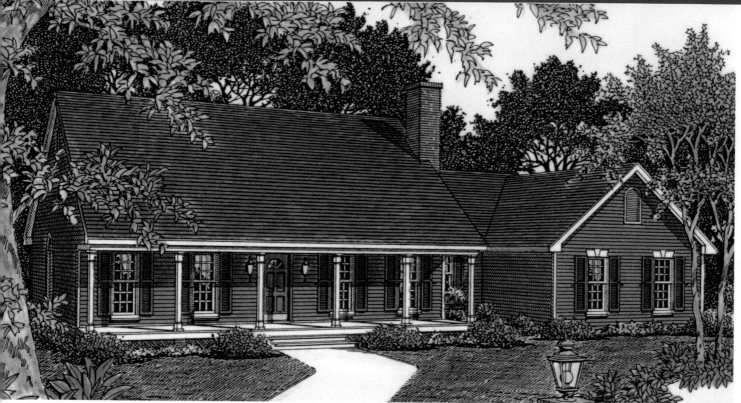

This charming three-bedroom Colonial home fits equally well in an urban or rural setting. The inviting front porch opens to the spacious great room where the grand fireplace sets a heartwarming mood. To the rear, the island kitchen is situated between the dining room and the sunroom—where casual meals can be served. The master suite, with its luxurious private bath, finds privacy on the right. And two family bedrooms share a Jack-and-Jill bath on the left.

plan# HPK0700077

Style: Cottage
Square Footage: 2,190
Bonus Space: 624 sq. ft.
Bedrooms: 3
Bathrooms: 2½
Width: 75' - 6"
Depth: 55' - 2"
Foundation: Crawlspace, Slab, Unfinished Basement

SEARCH ONLINE @ EPLANS.COM

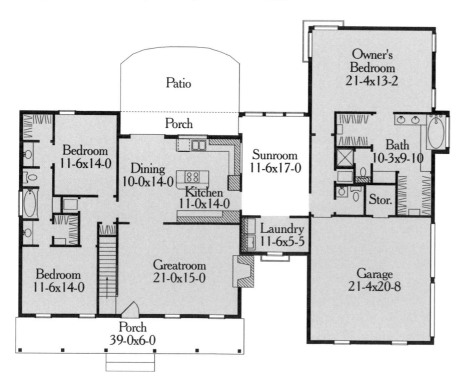

Elegant columns adorn the front porch of this plan and give it character. Though small in square footage, this home is designed for gracious living. The living and dining rooms are open and surround a galley-style kitchen with access to the two-car garage and its storage space. Bedrooms are on the right side of the plan and include a master suite and two family bedrooms. The master suite has a private bath with a compartmented tub and toilet. It also features a walk-in closet. Family bedrooms share a full hall bath.

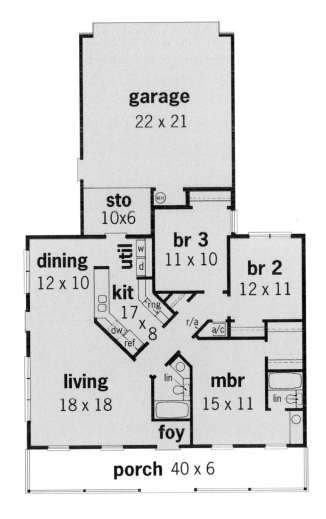

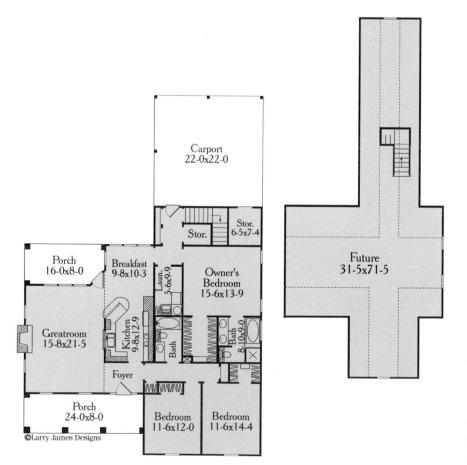

©Larry James Designs

plan# HPK0700079

Style: Country Cottage
Square Footage: 1,685
Bonus Space: 100 sq. ft.
Bedrooms: 3
Bathrooms: 2
Width: 48' - 0"
Depth: 72' - 0"
Foundation: Unfinished Basement, Crawlspace, Slab

SEARCH ONLINE @ EPLANS.COM

Designed for a small lot, this country cottage lives like a much larger home. The foyer splits to lead to two bedrooms and a full bath, or to the great room, flooded with natural light and warmed by a central fireplace. An angled kitchen provides a serving bar and a sunny breakfast nook with porch access extending the living space. Past the convenient laundry and storage areas, the master suite enjoys an oversize walk-in closet and a plush bath with dual sinks and a spa tub. Future space above the carport can be used as a home gym, office, playroom, or studio.

plan# HPK0700080

Style: Country Cottage
Square Footage: 1,079
Bedrooms: 2
Bathrooms: 1
Width: 34' - 0"
Depth: 34' - 0"
Foundation: Unfinished Basement

SEARCH ONLINE @ EPLANS.COM

This house plan is rich in efficiency and cottage-style living. A quaint covered porch charms visitors and offers an enchanting glimpse into the spacious living room through a beautiful front window. Kitchen counter space is in abundance for the family chef. The kitchen is open to a dining area, which accesses the rear of the home. The opposite side of the home is dedicated to the family sleeping quarters. The master bedroom enjoys twin windows overlooking the backyard. An additional bedroom has a window viewing the front of the property and shares a full hall bath with the master bedroom.

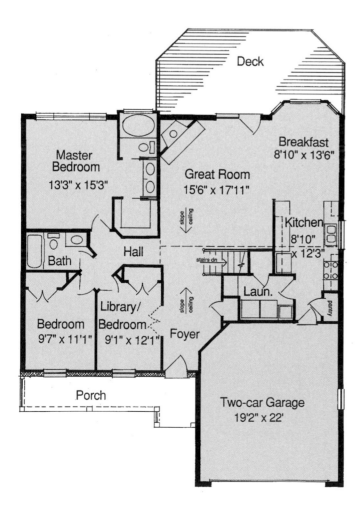

plan# HPK0700081

Style: Country Cottage
Square Footage: 1,422
Bedrooms: 3
Bathrooms: 2
Width: 45' - 0"
Depth: 51' - 4"
Foundation: Unfinished
Walkout Basement

SEARCH ONLINE @ EPLANS.COM

Homeowners can wait out rainy days on the front covered porch of this home and likewise enjoy sunny afternoons on the rear deck. They'll find spacious shelter inside in the large great room, easily accessible from the kitchen with a breakfast nook. With a corner fireplace and rear deck access, the great room will be buzzing with activity. Two secondary bedrooms—make one a library—share a full hall bath. The master suite is graciously appointed with a private bath and walk-in closet.

This cozy country cottage is enhanced with a front-facing planter box above the garage and a charming covered porch. The foyer leads to a vaulted great room, complete with a fireplace and radius windows. Decorative columns complement the entrance to the dining room, as does a decorative arch. The master suite includes a vaulted sitting room with a radius window.

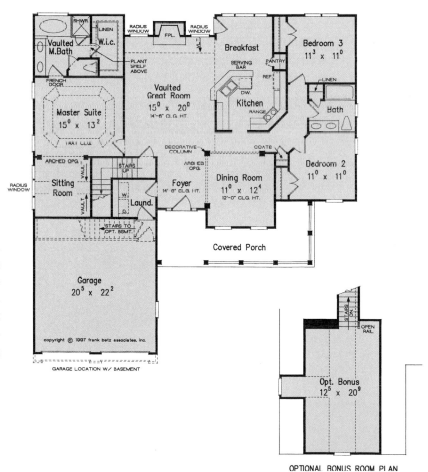

OPTIONAL BONUS ROOM PLAN

Welcome your family home to this wonderful four-bedroom cottage. Step through the entry door with its transom and sidelights to a well-lit foyer. A ribbon of windows greets the eye in the great room, and a fireplace spreads comfort. The master suite enjoys a private wing, luxurious bath, and His and Hers walk-in closets. On the opposite side of the plan, three secondary bedrooms share a full bath.

plan# HPK0700083

Style: Country Cottage
Square Footage: 2,093
Bedrooms: 4
Bathrooms: 2
Width: 71' - 2"
Depth: 56' - 4"
Foundation: Crawlspace, Slab, Unfinished Basement

SEARCH ONLINE @ EPLANS.COM

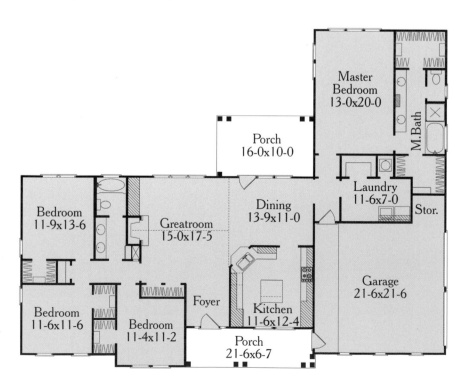

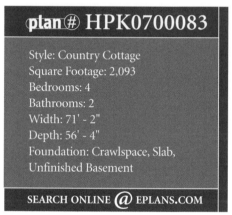

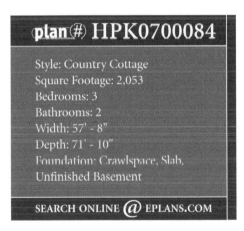

plan (#) HPK0700084

Style: Country Cottage
Square Footage: 2,053
Bedrooms: 3
Bathrooms: 2
Width: 57' - 8"
Depth: 71' - 10"
Foundation: Crawlspace, Slab,
Unfinished Basement

SEARCH ONLINE @ EPLANS.COM

Shutters, multipane glass windows and cross-hatched railing on the front porch make this a beautiful country cottage. To the left of the foyer is a roomy great room and a warming fireplace, framed by windows. To the right of the foyer, two family bedrooms feature walk-in closets and share a full bath. French doors, a fireplace and columns complete this three-bedroom design.

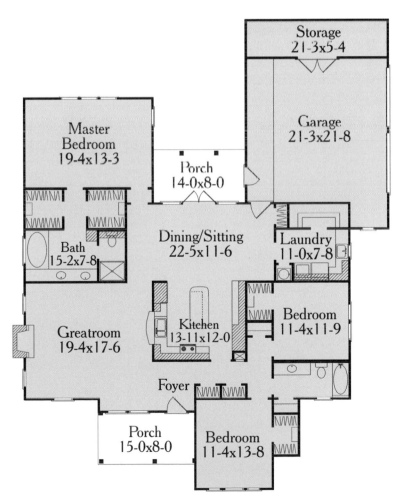

Storage
21-3x5-4

Garage
21-3x21-8

Master
Bedroom
19-4x13-3

Porch
14-0x8-0

Bath
15-2x7-8

Dining/Sitting
22-5x11-6

Laundry
11-0x7-8

Greatroom
19-4x17-6

Kitchen
13-11x12-0

Bedroom
11-4x11-9

Foyer

Porch
15-0x8-0

Bedroom
11-4x13-8

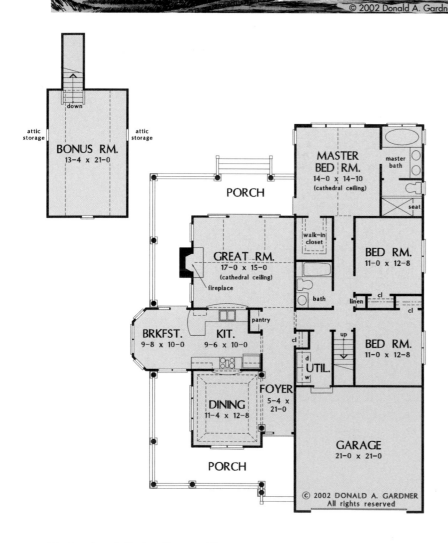

BONUS RM.
13-4 x 21-0

attic storage
attic storage

down

PORCH

MASTER BED RM.
14-0 x 14-10
(cathedral ceiling)

master bath

seat

GREAT RM.
17-0 x 15-0
(cathedral ceiling)

fireplace

walk-in closet

BED RM.
11-0 x 12-8

bath

cl
linen
cl

pantry

BRKFST.
9-8 x 10-0

KIT.
9-6 x 10-0

cl

up

BED RM.
11-0 x 12-8

UTIL.
d
w

DINING
11-4 x 12-8

FOYER
5-4 x 21-0

GARAGE
21-0 x 21-0

PORCH

plan# HPK0700085

Style: Cottage
Square Footage: 1,700
Bonus Space: 333 sq. ft.
Bedrooms: 3
Bathrooms: 2
Width: 49' - 0"
Depth: 65' - 4"

SEARCH ONLINE @ EPLANS.COM

This homespun traditional plan has a porch that goes on and on—and that's accessible from nearly every room in the house. Columns and fanlight windows dress up the facade; the interior offers a unique layout that's perfect for family living. The hearth-warmed great room is amplified by a cathedral ceiling, and it views the porch at the side and rear. The spacious kitchen, complete with pantry, opens to a bay-windowed breakfast nook that has a door to the porch. Three bedrooms make up the right wing's sleeping quarters, including two that share a full bath and access to the utility room. The deluxe master suite at the rear boasts a picture window, walk-in closet, elegant bath, and porch access. Upstairs, bonus space can become whatever kind of room you wish.

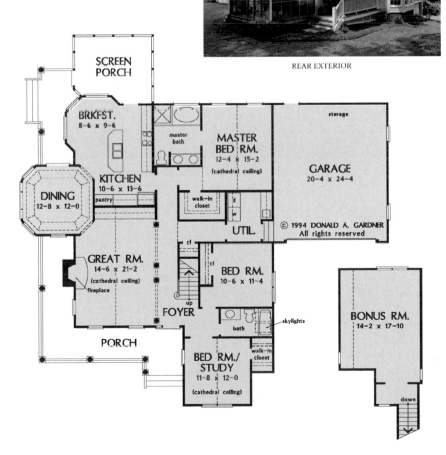

REAR EXTERIOR

plan# HPK0700086

Style: Cottage
Square Footage: 1,787
Bonus Space: 326 sq. ft.
Bedrooms: 3
Bathrooms: 2
Width: 66' - 2"
Depth: 66' - 8"

SEARCH ONLINE @ EPLANS.COM

Cathedral ceilings bring a feeling of spaciousness to this home. The great room features a fireplace, cathedral ceilings, and built-in bookshelves. The kitchen is designed for efficient use with its food preparation island and pantry. The master suite provides a welcome retreat with a cathedral ceiling, a walk-in closet, and a luxurious bath. Two additional bedrooms, one with a walk-in closet, share a skylit bath. A second-floor bonus room is perfect for a study or a play area.

SCREEN PORCH

BRKFST. 8-6 x 9-6

master bath

MASTER BED RM. 12-4 x 15-2 (cathedral ceiling)

storage

GARAGE 20-4 x 24-4

DINING 12-8 x 12-0

KITCHEN 10-6 x 13-6

pantry

walk-in closet

UTIL.

© 1994 DONALD A. GARDNER All rights reserved

GREAT RM. 14-6 x 21-2 (cathedral ceiling) fireplace

BED RM. 10-6 x 11-4

up

FOYER

PORCH

bath

skylights

BED RM./ STUDY 11-8 x 12-0 (cathedral ceiling)

walk-in closet

BONUS RM. 14-2 x 17-10

down

Here is a starter home that is quaint and cozy yet spacious—three bedrooms with bonus space on the second floor for future expansion. The double-door entry opens to the great room where a wall of windows looks out to the rear deck. The dining room with a sunny bay window sits beyond a dramatic arch to the right. The U-shaped kitchen adjoins the dining room with the utility and laundry rooms close at hand. The master suite offers privacy on the right while two family bedrooms share a full bath on the left.

plan# HPK0700087

Style: Country Cottage
Square Footage: 1,380
Bonus Space: 372 sq. ft.
Bedrooms: 3
Bathrooms: 2
Width: 48' - 0"
Depth: 43' - 4"
Foundation: Crawlspace, Slab, Unfinished Basement

SEARCH ONLINE @ EPLANS.COM

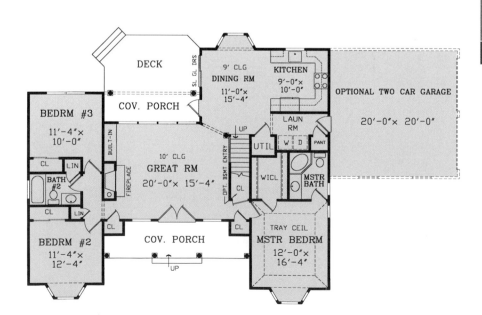

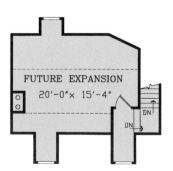

ORDER BLUEPRINTS 24 HOURS, 7 DAYS A WEEK, AT 1-800-521-6797

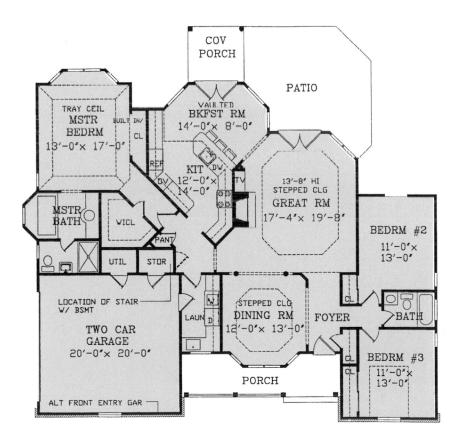

plan# HPK0700088

Style: Cottage
Square Footage: 1,860
Bedrooms: 3
Bathrooms: 2
Width: 57' - 4"
Depth: 49' - 8"
Foundation: Crawlspace, Slab,
Unfinished Basement

SEARCH ONLINE @ EPLANS.COM

Simple symmetry lends a feeling of cozy comfort, but don't be fooled by the facade. This home packs a wallop—stepped ceilings in the dining and great rooms, vaulted ceiling in the breakfast room adjoining the angled galley kitchen, French-door access to the covered rear porch and patio, and elegant columns and archways throughout. The secluded master suite is sure to please with a large walk-in closet, tray ceiling, bay window, garden tub, and compartmented shower and toilet. Two family bedrooms on the right share a full bath.

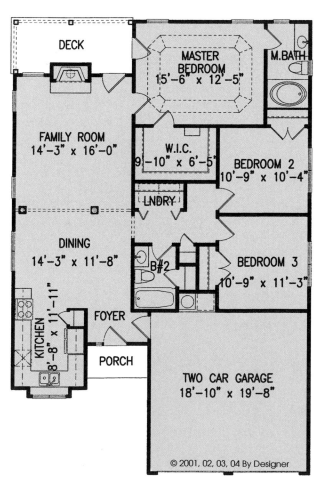

plan# HPK0700089

Style: Country Cottage
Square Footage: 1,277
Bedrooms: 3
Bathrooms: 2
Width: 36' - 0"
Depth: 55' - 0"
Foundation: Slab

SEARCH ONLINE @ EPLANS.COM

Three gables welcome you to this handsome three-bedroom bungalow. Inside columns separate the living and dining rooms yet allow a sense of spacious openness. The well-equipped kitchen opens easily into the dining area and a rear patio can be entered from the living room. On the right side of the home, three bedrooms...one a master suite with a private bath...provide sleeping quarters. A handy laundry and a two-car, front-loading garage complete the plan.

SECOND FLOOR

FIRST FLOOR

plan # HPK0700090

Style: Country Cottage
First Floor: 680 sq. ft.
Second Floor: 388 sq. ft.
Total: 1,068 sq. ft.
Bedrooms: 3
Bathrooms: 2
Width: 24' - 0"
Depth: 30' - 0"
Foundation: Unfinished Basement

SEARCH ONLINE @ EPLANS.COM

This charming and romantic cottage design is great as a second home or for a growing family. A quaint, covered porch wraps around one side of the home—perfect for rocking chairs on lazy summer days. Double doors open directly into the kitchen/dining area. A staircase to the second floor overlooks the open family room. The first-floor bedroom is located close to the hall shower bath. Upstairs, two additional family bedrooms share a full hall bath.

© 2002 Donald A. Gardner, Inc.

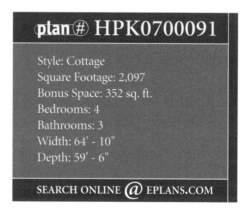

plan # HPK0700091

Style: Cottage
Square Footage: 2,097
Bonus Space: 352 sq. ft.
Bedrooms: 4
Bathrooms: 3
Width: 64' - 10"
Depth: 59' - 6"

SEARCH ONLINE @ EPLANS.COM

SCREEN PORCH
25-10 x 9-4

BRKFST.
11-8 x 8-10
(cathedral ceiling)

MASTER BED RM.
16-2 x 13-8

fireplace

GREAT RM.
19-0 x 15-8
(cathedral ceiling)

KIT.
11-8 x 12-4

bath

BED RM.
11-0 x 12-0

walk-in closet   walk-in closet

cl

cl

master bath   bath

FOYER
6-0 x 11-0

cl

DINING
11-0 x 13-0

UTIL.
6-0 x 10-4

up

w
d

BED RM.
11-8 x 11-8

cl

BED RM./ STUDY
11-4 x 12-10
(cathedral ceiling)

PORCH

GARAGE
21-8 x 21-0

STORAGE

down

attic storage

BONUS RM.
14-4 x 21-0

attic storage

Random stonework and wood
siding bring country flavor to this sweet country cottage. From the foyer, columns announce the great room, highlighted by a cathedral ceiling, screened-porch access and a fireplace with surrounding built-ins. Cathedral ceilings also grace the kitchen and breakfast area, as well as the front bedroom/study. On the far right, two bedrooms share a full bath; on the far left, the master suite will surely impress.

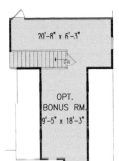

© 2003, Garrell Associates, Inc.

plan # HPK0700092

Style: Country Cottage
Square Footage: 1,656
Bonus Space: 368 sq. ft.
Bedrooms: 3
Bathrooms: 2
Width: 50' - 0"
Depth: 48' - 0"
Foundation: Slab

SEARCH ONLINE @ EPLANS.COM

Small Arts and Crafts details enhance this ranch-style home. Designed using open space and natural traffic flow for an unobstructed layout that includes: split bedrooms, an efficient yet spacious kitchen with bumped-out breakfast nook, and a dining room oriented to take advantage of the corner fireplace in the grand room. The master suite introduces itself with double doors and enjoys a private bath and walk-in closet.

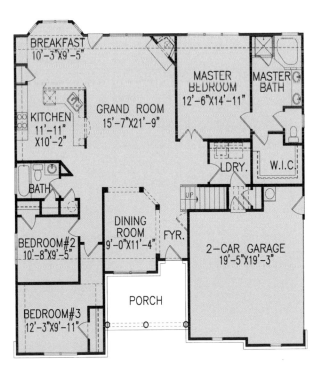

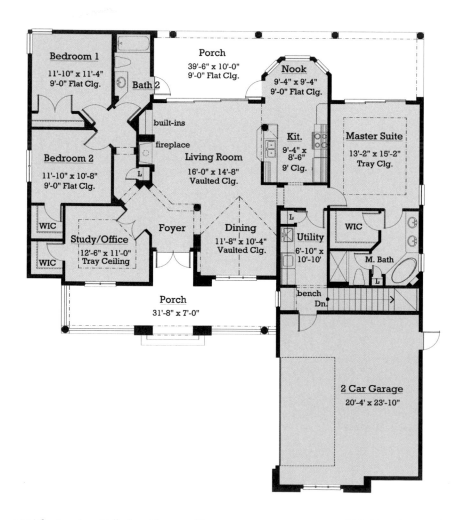

ptan# HPK0700093

Style: Cottage
Square Footage: 1,822
Bedrooms: 3
Bathrooms: 2
Width: 58' - 0"
Depth: 67' - 2"
Foundation: Unfinished Basement

SEARCH ONLINE @ EPLANS.COM

Stone bays and wood siding make up the exterior facade on this one-story home. The interior revolves around the living room with an attached dining room and the galley kitchen with a breakfast room. The master suite has a fine bath and a walk-in closet. One of three family bedrooms on the left side of the plan could be used as a home office.

plan # HPK0700094

Style: Country Cottage
Square Footage: 1,098
Bedrooms: 2
Bathrooms: 1
Width: 46' - 0"
Depth: 40' - 4"
Foundation: Unfinished Basement

SEARCH ONLINE @ EPLANS.COM

This two-bedroom home borrows heavily from the European traditions with its hipped roof, keystone arches and the winged wall on the single-car garage. Inside, a family room is located immediately to the left. The combined kitchen/dining area is spacious enough for casual gatherings. A rear porch is accessible through the sliding glass doors of the dining area. The large master bedroom and additional family bedroom across the hall share a full hall bath with a corner whirlpool tub and a separate shower.

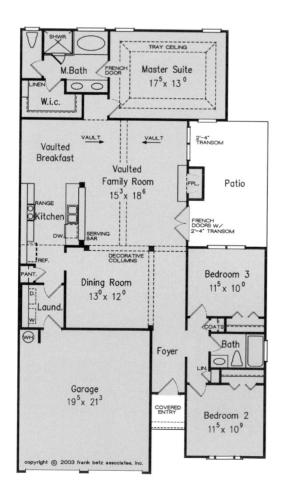

copyright © 2003 frank betz associates, inc.

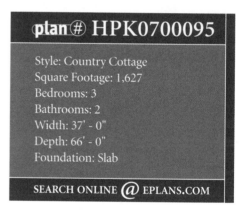

plan # HPK0700095

Style: Country Cottage
Square Footage: 1,627
Bedrooms: 3
Bathrooms: 2
Width: 37' - 0"
Depth: 66' - 0"
Foundation: Slab

SEARCH ONLINE @ EPLANS.COM

This easy-living design offers plenty of open spaces and height without sacrificing function. A laundry and utility room placed near the kitchen ensures quiet enjoyment for those in the bedroom. The continuous breakfast nook and family room allows for quiet in the master suite, where a tray ceiling, large walk-in closet, compartmented toilet, and whirlpool tub make this suite a private retreat.

ORDER BLUEPRINTS 24 HOURS, 7 DAYS A WEEK, AT 1-800-521-6797

plan# HPK0700096

Style: Country Cottage
First Floor: 1,704 sq. ft.
Second Floor: 734 sq. ft.
Total: 2,438 sq. ft.
Bonus Space: 479 sq. ft.
Bedrooms: 3
Bathrooms: 3½
Width: 50' - 0"
Depth: 82' - 6"
Foundation: Crawlspace

SEARCH ONLINE @ EPLANS.COM

Elegant country—that's one way to describe this attractive three-bedroom home. Inside, comfort is evidently the theme, with the formal dining room flowing into the U-shaped kitchen and casual dining taking place in the sunny breakfast area. The spacious, vaulted great room offers a fireplace and built-ins. The first-floor master suite is complete with a walk-in closet, a whirlpool tub, and a separate shower. Upstairs, the sleeping quarters include two family bedrooms with private baths and walk-in closets.

SECOND FLOOR

FIRST FLOOR

Quaint and sensible from the front, this spacious plan will surprise you with its fun, vacation-style design. A true wraparound deck begins at the front entrance and sweeps around to the rear with a deck-like jut. Inside, living areas are flooded with natural light, courtesy of French doors and floor-to-ceiling windows. Ample counter space in the kitchen makes it a chef's delight, and the sunlit dining room makes for pleasant meals year-round. Bedrooms are separated by a luxurious bath; the master bedroom enjoys an interesting shape and convenient porch access. The lower level is available for expansion as your family grows.

plan# HPK0700097

Style: Cottage
Square Footage: 1,056
Bedrooms: 2
Bathrooms: 1
Width: 39' - 8"
Depth: 36' - 4"
Foundation: Unfinished Basement

SEARCH ONLINE @ EPLANS.COM

3,30 X 3,90
11'-0" X 13'-0"

3,00 X 3,30
10'-0" X 11'-0"

5,70 X 3,60
19'-0" X 12'-0"

3,20 X 2,70
10'-8" X 9'-0"

3,20 X 3,00
10'-8" X 10'-0"

FRONT EXTERIOR

ORDER BLUEPRINTS 24 HOURS, 7 DAYS A WEEK, AT 1-800-521-6797

© 2002 Donald A. Gardner, Inc.

plan# HPK0700098

Style: Cottage
Square Footage: 1,952
Bonus Space: 339 sq. ft.
Bedrooms: 4
Bathrooms: 3
Width: 50' - 0"
Depth: 60' - 0"

SEARCH ONLINE @ EPLANS.COM

As at home in your neighborhood as it is in the country, this design combines traditional charm with Craftsman appeal. Twin Palladian windows and a flower box invite you to enter; a great room with a fireplace and a dining room defined by decorative columns await. The kitchen opens to the breakfast area for an airy effect. The sumptuous vaulted master suite will be a welcome retreat. Two additional bedrooms share a full bath. Bonus space above the garage is limited only by your imagination.

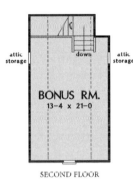

BONUS RM.
13-4 x 21-0

SECOND FLOOR

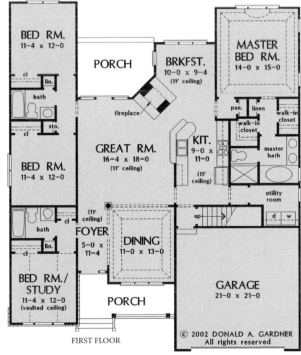

FIRST FLOOR

© 2002 DONALD A. GARDNER
All rights reserved

OPT. Bedroom 4
12⁰ x 14⁵

Great Room Below

VAULT

Bath

OPEN RAIL
STAIRS DN.

Foyer Below

VAULT

Attic Space

Covered Porch

FRENCH DOOR

FPL.

VAULT

Dining Room
12⁰ x 11⁸

Vaulted Family Room
17⁰ x 18⁸

VAULT

Vaulted Master Suite
12⁰ x 15⁰

VAULT

Vaulted M.Bath

SHWR

LINEN

W.i.c.

SERVING BAR

DW.

RANGE

Kitchen

REF.

PANTRY

W.

D.

STAIRS DN.

OPEN RAIL

STAIRS UP

Storage

Vaulted Foyer

COATS

Bath

LINEN

Bedroom 2
11⁰ x 10⁴

Bedroom 3
12⁰ x 10⁶

COVERED ENTRY

Garage
20⁵ x 19⁸

plan# HPK0700099

Style: Country Cottage
Square Footage: 1,477
Bonus Space: 283 sq. ft.
Bedrooms: 3
Bathrooms: 2
Width: 51' - 0"
Depth: 51' - 4"
Foundation: Crawlspace,
Unfinished Walkout Basement

SEARCH ONLINE @ EPLANS.COM

This adorable three-bedroom home will provide a pleasant atmosphere for your family. The communal living areas reside on the left side of the plan. The L-shaped kitchen includes a serving bar, which opens to the dining area. The vaulted family room features a fireplace and leads to the sleeping quarters. A master suite and vaulted master bath will pamper homeowners. Two family bedrooms reside across the hall and share a full hall bath. Upstairs, an optional fourth bedroom and full bath are perfect for guests.

plan# HPK0700100

Style: Country Cottage
Square Footage: 1,328
Bedrooms: 3
Bathrooms: 2
Width: 40' - 0"
Depth: 52' - 0"
Foundation: Slab

SEARCH ONLINE @ EPLANS.COM

This compact home has a lot more packed inside its walls than it might appear from the outside. It enjoys three bedrooms, one of them an amenity-filled master suite; two baths; a well-equipped laundry; and a two-car garage. The grand room, with a warming fireplace, soars two stories high to a vaulted ceiling. It easily opens to the kitchen and a breakfast nook, which opens to a rear deck or patio.

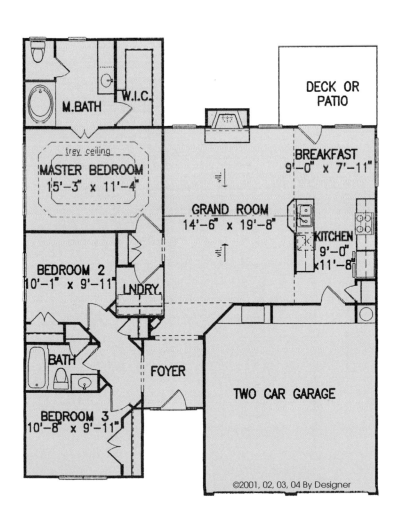

©2001, 02, 03, 04 By Designer

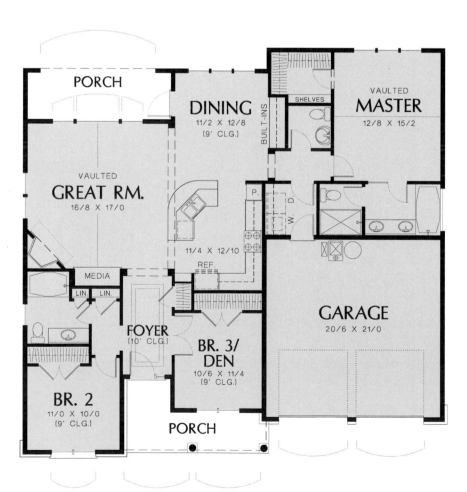

PORCH

DINING
11/2 X 12/8
(9' CLG.)

SHELVES

VAULTED
MASTER
12/8 X 15/2

BUILT-INS

VAULTED
GREAT RM.
16/8 X 17/0

11/4 X 12/10

P.

W. D.

REF.

MEDIA

LIN. LIN.

FOYER
(10' CLG.)

**BR. 3/
DEN**
10/6 X 11/4
(9' CLG.)

GARAGE
20/6 X 21/0

BR. 2
11/0 X 10/0
(9' CLG.)

PORCH

plan # HPK0700101

Style: Country Cottage
Square Footage: 1,580
Bedrooms: 3
Bathrooms: 2½
Width: 50' - 0"
Depth: 48' - 0"
Foundation: Crawlspace

SEARCH ONLINE @ EPLANS.COM

This charming one-story plan features a facade that is accented by a stone pediment and a shed-dormer window. Inside, elegant touches grace the efficient floor plan. Vaulted ceilings adorn the great room and master bedroom, and a 10-foot tray ceiling highlights the foyer. One of the front bedrooms makes a perfect den; another accesses a full hall bath with a linen closet. The great room, which opens to the porch, includes a fireplace and a media niche. The dining room offers outdoor access and built-ins for ultimate convenience.

Peek-a-boo gables stir up the country appeal of this home. A front porch opens through the foyer to the spacious dining room, great room and gallery hall. A fireplace flanked by built-ins and three sets of double French doors to the rear porch enhance the great room. The kitchen work harmoniously with a breakfast nook to whip up casual meals fast. The master bedroom sits on the left side for privacy. Two family bedrooms are to the far right of the plan and share a full compartmented bath.

An arched clerestory window, strikingly prominent on the front, cascades the two-story foyer of this country cottage with natural light. Elegant meals will feel natural in the dining room with its grand octagonal-shaped stepped ceiling. Columns define this area from the great room, which enjoys an extended-hearth fireplace and extensive built-in cabinets and shelves. A snack counter separates the great room from the kitchen. A window seat adds that extra touch to make the lavish master suite something above the ordinary. Other amenities include a beautiful bell-shaped tub, shower, double-sink vanity, and twin walk-in closets. On the other side of the house two more bedrooms share a bath.

plan# HPK0700103

Style: Country Cottage
Square Footage: 1,892
Bonus Space: 285 sq. ft.
Bedrooms: 3
Bathrooms: 2½
Width: 65' - 4"
Depth: 45' - 10"
Foundation: Crawlspace, Slab, Unfinished Basement

SEARCH ONLINE @ EPLANS.COM

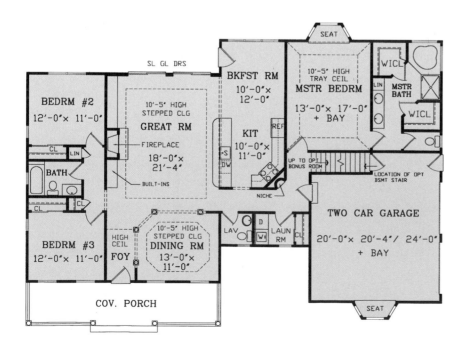

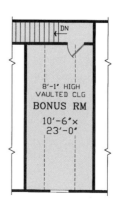

ORDER BLUEPRINTS 24 HOURS, 7 DAYS A WEEK, AT 1-800-521-6797

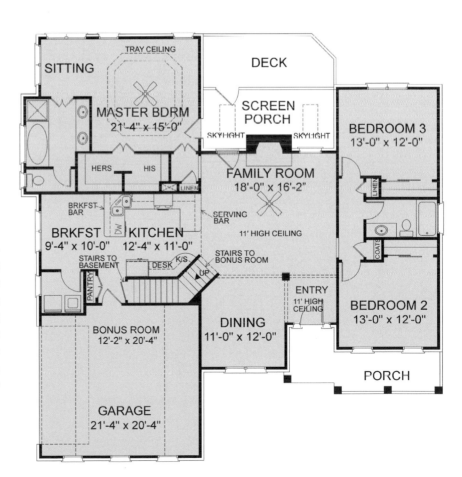

plan # HPK0700104

Style: Cottage
Square Footage: 1,787
Bonus Space: 263 sq. ft.
Bedrooms: 3
Bathrooms: 2
Width: 55' - 8"
Depth: 56' 6"
Foundation: Unfinished Walkout
Basement, Slab, Crawlspace

SEARCH ONLINE @ EPLANS.COM

This striking and distinctive ranch home includes all the frills. From the inviting front porch to the screened porch and deck, this home provides dramatic spaces, luxurious appointments and spacious living areas. Soaring ceilings enhance the entryway. To the left is the dining room—open to the entry and family room. The kitchen is open and provides both a breakfast and serving bar. The dramatic master suite is loaded with amenities.

plan# HPK0700105

Style: Country Cottage
Square Footage: 2,151
Bedrooms: 3
Bathrooms: 2
Width: 61' - 0"
Depth: 55' - 8"
Foundation: Crawlspace,
Unfinished Basement

SEARCH ONLINE @ EPLANS.COM

This home maintains true country ambiance, while achieving a very modern layout. Shuttered windows and porch details add charm to the facade. Enter the large foyer to find a formal dining room to the right and a sophisticated gallery hall straight ahead. The great room lies just beyond, complete with built-in shelves, a fireplace, and views of the rear property. The adjacent bayed breakfast nook is open to a counter-filled kitchen. Two family bedrooms share a full bath; the stunning master suite enjoys its own luxurious bath on the right. Upstairs, a wealth of future expansion space awaits.

VICTORIANS

Among the most popular and recognizable architectural styles in America is the Victorian home, noteworthy for its steep roofs, intricately detailed woodworking, and the trademark turrets of the later styles. Most popular during the latter half of the 19th Century, today's Victorians celebrate the grace and beauty of that period while incorporating modern amenities and free-flowing layouts.

Rapid industrialization allowed easier access to the complex shapes and styles that defined Victorian homes. Modern Victorians capture that external beauty and combine it with floor plans that fit today's lifestyles. Large open spaces typically dominate the main level, with great rooms that connect gracefully with kitchens, breakfast areas, and more.

The unique shapes and sizes of Victorian homes also provide perfect spots for quiet getaways in your home. You'll find clever spots for home offices or guest bedrooms, often utilizing the towers that are common in Victorian homes, especially in the Queen Anne style. The large porches also offer comfortable spots for outdoor dining or a porch swing. ■

The distinctive tower in Design HPK0700121 is home to the master bathroom on the second floor, a perfect spot for a whirlpool tub. See page 133 for more.

This lovely Victorian home has a perfect balance of ornamental features making it irresistible, yet affordable. The beveled-glass front door invites you into a roomy foyer. The open kitchen and breakfast room and abundant counter space make cooking a pleasure. The upper level includes a master suite with a multifaceted vaulted ceiling, a separate shower, and a six-foot garden tub. Two additional bedrooms share a conveniently located bath.

plan# HPK0700106

Style: Victorian
First Floor: 812 sq. ft.
Second Floor: 786 sq. ft.
Total: 1,598 sq. ft.
Bedrooms: 3
Bathrooms: 2½
Width: 52' - 0"
Depth: 28' - 0"
Foundation: Slab, Crawlspace

SEARCH ONLINE @ EPLANS.COM

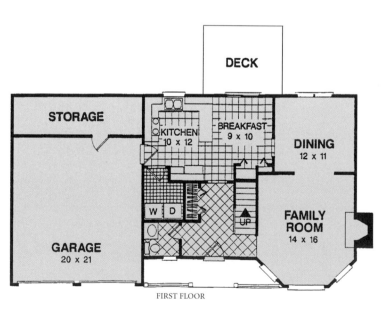

FIRST FLOOR

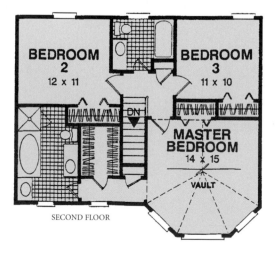

SECOND FLOOR

ORDER BLUEPRINTS 24 HOURS, 7 DAYS A WEEK, AT 1-800-521-6797

plan # HPK0700107

Style: Victorian
First Floor: 1,600 sq. ft.
Second Floor: 790 sq. ft.
Total: 2,390 sq. ft.
Bedrooms: 4
Bathrooms: 3½
Width: 45' - 0"
Depth: 54' - 0"
Foundation: Crawlspace

SEARCH ONLINE @ EPLANS.COM

Queen Anne houses, with their projecting bays, towers, and wraparound porches, are the apex of the Victorian era. This up-to-date rendition of the beloved style captures a floor plan that is as dramatic on the inside as it is on the outside. The front-facing pediment ornamented with typical gable detailing highlights the front doorway and provides additional welcome to this enchanted abode. The angles and bays that occur in every first-floor room add visual excitement to formal and informal living and dining areas. A well-lit breakfast bay with its soaring ceiling is a spectacular addition to this classic plan. The first-floor master suite features two walk-in closets. Three upstairs bedrooms also have spacious walk-in closets.

SECOND FLOOR

FIRST FLOOR

SECOND FLOOR

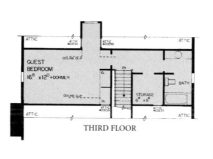

THIRD FLOOR

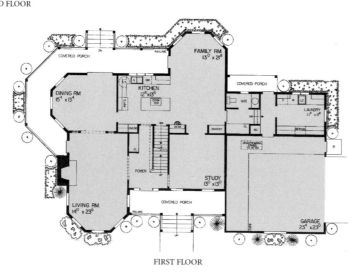

FIRST FLOOR

plan # HPK0700108

Style: Victorian **LD**
First Floor: 1,618 sq. ft.
Second Floor: 1,315 sq. ft.
Third Floor: 477 sq. ft.
Total: 3,410 sq. ft.
Bedrooms: 4
Bathrooms: 3½
Width: 71' - 8"
Foundation: Unfinished Basement

SEARCH ONLINE @ EPLANS.COM

This delicately detailed exterior houses an outstanding family-oriented floor plan. The efficient kitchen, with its island cooking station, functions well with the dining and family rooms. A study provides a quiet first-floor haven for the family's less-active pursuits. Upstairs, there are three big bedrooms and a fine master bath. The third floor provides a guest suite and huge bulk storage area. This house has a basement for the development of further recreational and storage facilities.

plan# HPK0700109

Style: Victorian
First Floor: 2,506 sq. ft.
Second Floor: 2,315 sq. ft.
Total: 4,821 sq. ft.
Bonus Space: 278 sq. ft.
Bedrooms: 5
Bathrooms: 4
Width: 60' - 0"
Depth: 97' - 0"
Foundation: Crawlspace

SEARCH ONLINE @ EPLANS.COM

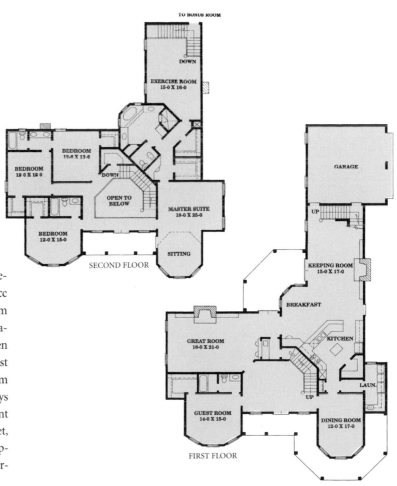

The lacy veranda that embraces the exterior of this Queen Anne home offers outdoor living space under its shady recesses. The first floor enjoys a guest room with a private bath and walk-in closet. A great room features a fireplace, built-in shelves, and a wet bar. The kitchen boasts a walk-in pantry, an island countertop, a breakfast nook with a bayed window, and access to the keeping room and to the rear covered porch. The second floor enjoys three family bedrooms and the master suite. The elegant master suite features a sitting area located within a turret, a spacious walk-in closet, an enormous bath with a step-up tub and dual vanities, and access to its own private exercise room. This home comes with a two-car garage.

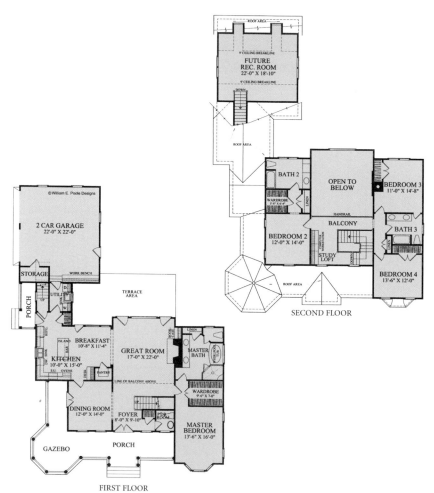

FIRST FLOOR

SECOND FLOOR

2 CAR GARAGE
22'-0" X 22'-0"

©William E. Poole Designs

STORAGE
WORK BENCH

PORCH

UTILITY

TERRACE AREA

BREAKFAST
10'-8" X 11'-4"

KITCHEN
10'-0" X 15'-0"

ISLAND

S.I. OVENS

DESK

PANTRY

GREAT ROOM
17'-0" X 22'-0"

LINEN

MASTER BATH

LINE OF BALCONY ABOVE

WARDROBE
9'-6" X 7-0"

DINING ROOM
12'-0" X 14'-0"

FOYER
8'-0" X 9'-10"

POWDER ROOM

MASTER BEDROOM
13'-6" X 16'-0"

GAZEBO

PORCH

FUTURE REC. ROOM
22'-0" X 18'-10"

9' CEILING BREAKLINE

ROOF AREA

DOWN

ROOF AREA

BATH 2

OPEN TO BELOW

BEDROOM 3
11'-0" X 14'-8"

WARDROBE
9'-6" X 4'-4"

LINEN

BALCONY

HANDRAIL

BEDROOM 2
12'-0" X 14'-0"

STUDY LOFT

BATH 3

DOWN

BEDROOM 4
13'-6" X 12'-0"

ROOF AREA

plan # HPK0700110

Style: Victorian
First Floor: 1,734 sq. ft.
Second Floor: 1,091 sq. ft.
Total: 2,825 sq. ft.
Bonus Space: 488 sq. ft.
Bedrooms: 4
Bathrooms: 3½
Width: 57' - 6"
Depth: 80' - 11"
Foundation: Crawlspace,
Unfinished Basement

SEARCH ONLINE @ EPLANS.COM

Wonderful Victorian charm combines with the flavor of country in this delightful two-story home. A wraparound porch with a gazebo corner welcomes you into the foyer, where the formal dining room waits to the left and a spacious, two-story great room is just ahead. Here, a fireplace, built-ins, and backyard access add to the charm. The L-shaped kitchen features a work-top island, a walk-in pantry, and a breakfast area. Located on the first floor for privacy, the master suite offers a large walk-in closet and a pampering bath. Upstairs, three bedrooms—one with a private bath—share access to a study loft.

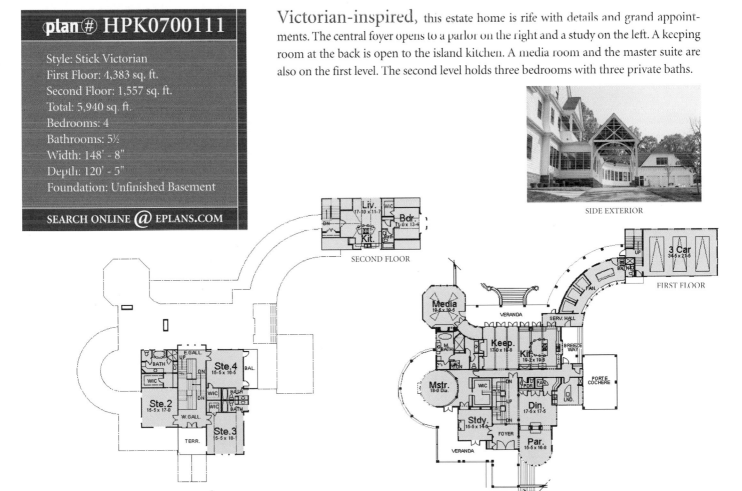

plan# HPK0700111

Style: Stick Victorian
First Floor: 4,383 sq. ft.
Second Floor: 1,557 sq. ft.
Total: 5,940 sq. ft.
Bedrooms: 4
Bathrooms: 5½
Width: 148' - 8"
Depth: 120' - 5"
Foundation: Unfinished Basement

SEARCH ONLINE @ EPLANS.COM

Victorian-inspired, this estate home is rife with details and grand appointments. The central foyer opens to a parlor on the right and a study on the left. A keeping room at the back is open to the island kitchen. A media room and the master suite are also on the first level. The second level holds three bedrooms with three private baths.

SIDE EXTERIOR

Country Victoriana embellishes this beautiful home. Perfect for a corner lot, this home begs for porch swings and lemonade. Inside, extra-high ceilings expand the space, as a thoughtful floor plan invites family and friends. The two-story great room enjoys a warming fireplace and wonderful rear views. The country kitchen has a preparation island and easily serves the sunny bayed nook and the formal dining room. To the far left, a bedroom serves as a perfect guest room; to the far right, a turret houses a private den. Upstairs, two bedrooms (one in a turret) share a full bath and ample bonus space. The master suite opens through French doors to reveal a grand bedroom and a sumptuous bath with a bumped-out spa tub.

plan# HPK0700112

Style: Victorian
First Floor: 1,464 sq. ft.
Second Floor: 1,054 sq. ft.
Total: 2,518 sq. ft.
Bonus Space: 332 sq. ft.
Bedrooms: 4
Bathrooms: 3
Width: 59' - 0"
Depth: 51' - 6"
Foundation: Crawlspace

SEARCH ONLINE @ EPLANS.COM

FIRST FLOOR

SECOND FLOOR

plan # HPK0700113

Style: Victorian
First Floor: 2,099 sq. ft.
Second Floor: 1,260 sq. ft.
Total: 3,359 sq. ft.
Bonus Space: 494 sq. ft.
Bedrooms: 4
Bathrooms: 3½
Width: 68' - 4"
Depth: 54' - 0"
Foundation: Crawlspace

SEARCH ONLINE @ EPLANS.COM

This colonial home gets a Victorian treatment with an expansive covered porch complete with a gazebo-like terminus. Inside, the impressive foyer is flanked by the living room and the formal dining room. The spacious island kitchen is ideally situated between the dining room and the sunny breakfast area. Completing the living area, the family room enjoys a fireplace, built-ins, and a generous view. The lavish master suite resides on the far right with a private bath and a huge walk-in closet. A second master suite is found on the upper level along with two additional bedrooms, which share a full bath.

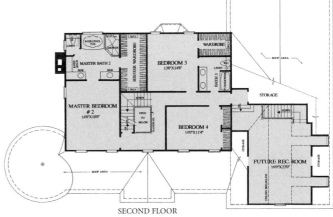

SECOND FLOOR

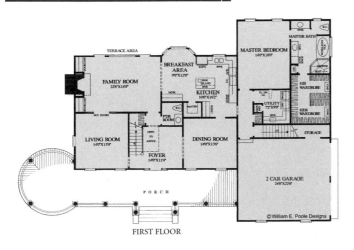

FIRST FLOOR

This farmhouse is resplendent with Victorian detailing, from the pinnacle to the circular porch. The large dining room boasts a fabulous view to the front of the plan through a set of windows. Aspects of the family room that are sure to please include a fireplace and access to the rear covered porch. The kitchen area includes an island, nook, utility room, and bathroom. The first-floor master suite contains His and Hers walk-in closets and dual vanities. Upstairs, three bedrooms share two full baths, and a bonus room completes the plan. The second-floor balcony looks to the family room below.

plan# HPK0700114

Style: Victorian
First Floor: 2,041 sq. ft.
Second Floor: 1,098 sq. ft.
Total: 3,139 sq. ft.
Bonus Space: 385 sq. ft.
Bedrooms: 4
Bathrooms: 3½
Width: 76' - 6"
Depth: 62' - 2"
Foundation: Slab

SEARCH ONLINE @ EPLANS.COM

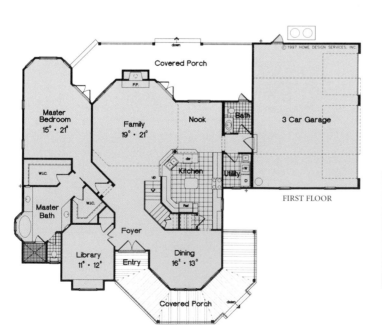

FIRST FLOOR

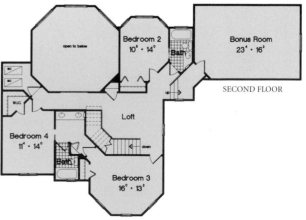

SECOND FLOOR

ORDER BLUEPRINTS 24 HOURS, 7 DAYS A WEEK, AT 1-800-521-6797

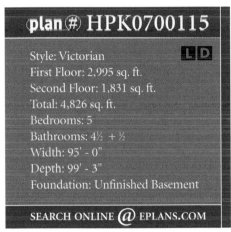

plan # HPK0700115

LD

Style: Victorian
First Floor: 2,995 sq. ft.
Second Floor: 1,831 sq. ft.
Total: 4,826 sq. ft.
Bedrooms: 5
Bathrooms: 4½ + ½
Width: 95' - 0"
Depth: 99' - 3"
Foundation: Unfinished Basement

SEARCH ONLINE @ EPLANS.COM

A magnificent, finely wrought covered porch wraps around this impressive Victorian estate home. The two-story foyer provides a direct view past the stylish banister into the great room, which has a large central fireplace. To the left of the foyer is a library and to the right is an octagonal-shaped dining room. The island cooktop completes the kitchen. A luxurious master suite on the first floor opens to the rear covered porch.

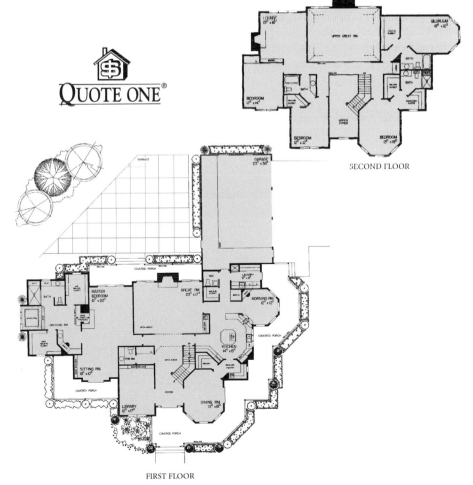

QUOTE ONE®

SECOND FLOOR

FIRST FLOOR

A two-story bay, a turret, and a wraparound porch create an eye-catching Victorian exterior. Inside, the parlor and the dining room are ideally situated for easy entertaining. Family and guests will delight in the gathering room, with its fireplace and built-in bookcases. The breakfast room offers sliding glass doors to the backyard as well as a pantry, a desk, and a nearby powder room. Upstairs, the skylit master suite pampers with a walk-in closet, a whirlpool tub, and dual sinks. Three family bedrooms share a large bath and a hall linen closet. Laundry facilities are also on this level.

plan # HPK0700116

Style: Victorian
First Floor: 1,054 sq. ft.
Second Floor: 1,262 sq. ft.
Total: 2,316 sq. ft.
Bedrooms: 4
Bathrooms: 2½
Width: 54' - 0"
Depth: 34' - 8"

SEARCH ONLINE @ EPLANS.COM

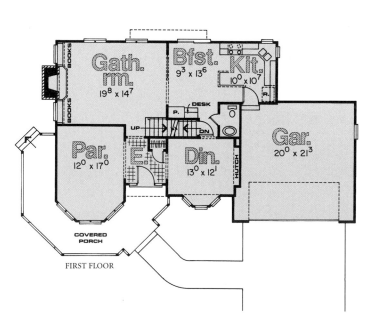

FIRST FLOOR

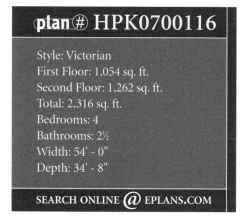

SECOND FLOOR

ORDER BLUEPRINTS 24 HOURS, 7 DAYS A WEEK, AT 1-800-521-6797

plan(#) HPK0700117

L D

Style: Victorian
First Floor: 1,186 sq. ft.
Second Floor: 988 sq. ft.
Total: 2,174 sq. ft.
Bedrooms: 4
Bathrooms: 2½
Width: 72' - 4"
Depth: 51' - 2"
Foundation: Unfinished Basement

SEARCH ONLINE @ EPLANS.COM

This Victorian-style exterior—a wraparound porch, mullion windows, and turret-style bays—offers a wonderful floor plan. More than just a pretty face, the turret houses a secluded study on the first level and provides a sunny bay window for a family bedroom upstairs. The second-level master suite boasts its own fireplace, a dressing area with a walk-in closet, and a lavish bath with a garden tub and twin vanities. The two-car garage offers space for a workshop or extra storage.

SECOND FLOOR

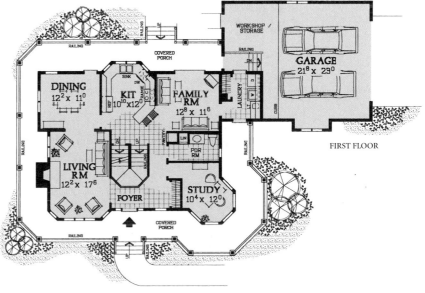

FIRST FLOOR

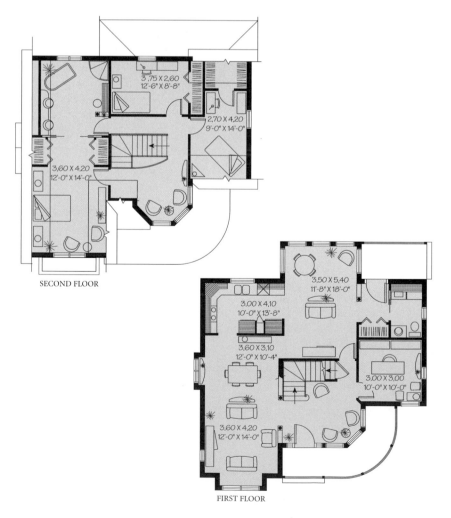

SECOND FLOOR

FIRST FLOOR

plan# HPK0700118

Style: Victorian
First Floor: 1,070 sq. ft.
Second Floor: 970 sq. ft.
Total: 2,040 sq. ft.
Bedrooms: 3
Bathrooms: 1½
Width: 36' - 0"
Depth: 40' - 8"
Foundation: Unfinished Basement

SEARCH ONLINE @ EPLANS.COM

Victorian styling can come in an affordable size, as this home shows. A sitting area inside the front hall connects with the family room for handling large parties. An enclosed room off the sitting area can be used as a study or extra bedroom. A combination half-bath and laundry is just inside the rear entrance for quick cleanup; the covered rear porch is accessed from a door just beyond the laundry area. For easy upkeep, the three bedrooms on the second floor share a full bath that includes a corner tub. One of the bedrooms offers access to a private balcony.

plan# HPK0700119

Style: Country Cottage
First Floor: 1,155 sq. ft.
Second Floor: 1,209 sq. ft.
Total: 2,364 sq. ft.
Bedrooms: 4
Bathrooms: 2½
Width: 46' - 0"
Depth: 36' - 8"
Foundation: Unfinished Basement

SEARCH ONLINE @ EPLANS.COM

With both farmhouse flavor and Victorian details, this plan features a wrap-around veranda and a bayed area on the first and second floors as well as a turret on the second floor. Inside, the living room's many windows pour light in. The dining area begins with a bay window and is conveniently near the kitchen and breakfast area—also with a bay window. The U-shaped kitchen features an island workstation, ensuring plenty of space for cooking projects. A nearby lavatory is available for guests. The family room has an eye-catching corner-set fireplace. Upstairs, three family bedrooms share a full hall bath, while the master suite has a private bath and balcony, a large walk-in closet, and a sitting alcove, placed within the turret.

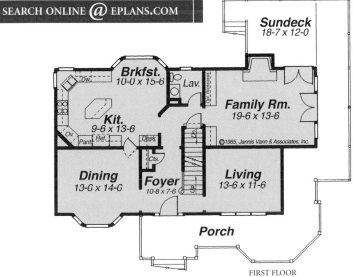

FIRST FLOOR

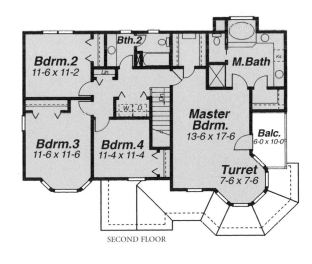

SECOND FLOOR

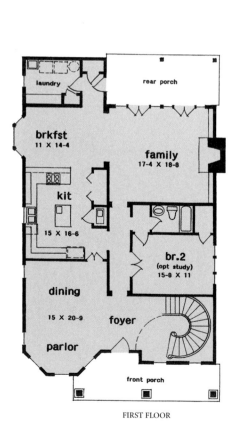

FIRST FLOOR

laundry

rear porch

brkfst
11 X 14-4

family
17-4 X 18-8

kit
15 X 16-6

br.2
(opt study)
15-8 X 11

dining
15 X 20-9

foyer

parlor

front porch

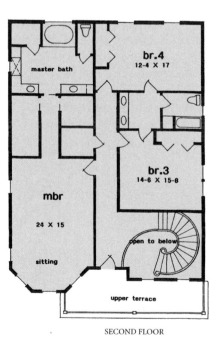

SECOND FLOOR

master bath

br.4
12-4 X 17

mbr
24 X 15

br.3
14-6 X 15-8

sitting

open to below

upper terrace

plan# HPK0700120

Style: Victorian
First Floor: 1,844 sq. ft.
Second Floor: 1,546 sq. ft.
Total: 3,390 sq. ft.
Bedrooms: 4
Bathrooms: 3
Width: 39' - 7"
Depth: 61' - 10"
Foundation: Slab

SEARCH ONLINE @ EPLANS.COM

Two porches and an upper terrace provide a variety of outside areas. The two-story cupola-style tower forms bay windows in the parlor near the formal dining room downstairs and in the sitting area in the master bedroom above. Four bedrooms, three bathrooms, and a well-designed kitchen complete this charming home.

plan# HPK0700121

Style: Victorian
First Floor: 1,266 sq. ft.
Second Floor: 1,482 sq. ft.
Total: 2,748 sq. ft.
Bedrooms: 3
Bathrooms: 2½
Width: 42' - 6"
Depth: 50' - 6"
Foundation: Crawlspace

SEARCH ONLINE @ EPLANS.COM

BEDROOM
12-0 X 16-0

BEDROOM
11-6 X 13-0

DOWN

MASTER
BEDROOM
13-0 X 17-0

SECOND FLOOR

LAUN.

BREAKFAST

GREAT ROOM
16-0 X 20-6

UP

ENTRY HALL

DINING ROOM
13-0 X 14-0

FIRST FLOOR

If you've dreamed about living in a classic Victorian home with all the modern amenities, this is the house for you. Complete with a front tower, a captain's deck, and a wraparound porch, this is an impressive plan. The two-story entry hallway leads into a comfortable living area that includes a great room with a fireplace flanked by windows. To the right, a kitchen that will delight any chef, if only for the ample counter space, is located between a dining room and breakfast area with a wall of windows. The upstairs master suite is regal in its grandeur. Most striking is the oversize tub located in the tower and surrounded by three windows. The master bedroom enjoys a bay window, also with three windows. Two other bedrooms share a bath.

FIRST FLOOR

SECOND FLOOR

This Victorian farmhouse is distinct because of its ornate detailing, including the decorative pinnacle, covered porch, and front-facing chimney. The living room is graced with a fireplace, wet bar, and tray ceiling. The family room also includes some appreciated amenities: an entertainment center, built-in bookshelves, and access to the covered patio. Upstairs, both the master suite and Bedroom 2 easily access a deck, and all bedrooms sport spacious walk-in closets. Ample attic space is also available for storage.

plan# HPK0700123

Design: HPK0700123
Style: Victorian
First Floor: 1,538 sq. ft.
Second Floor: 1,526 sq. ft.
Third Floor: 658 sq. ft.
Total: 3,722 sq. ft.
Bedrooms: 5
Bathrooms: 3½
Width: 67' - 0"
Foundation: Unfinished Basement

SEARCH ONLINE @ EPLANS.COM

This charming Victorian home is reminiscent of a time when letter writing was an art and the scent of lavender hung lightly in the air. However, the floor plan moves quickly into the present with a contemporary flair. A veranda wraps around the living room, providing entrance from each side. The hub of the first floor is a kitchen that serves the dining room, the family room, and the living room with equal ease. Located on the second floor are two family bedrooms, a full bath, and an opulent master suite. Amenities in this suite include a fireplace, a bay-windowed sitting room, a pampering master bath, and a private sundeck. The third floor holds two bedrooms—one a possible study—and a full bath.

THIRD FLOOR

QUOTE ONE®

SECOND FLOOR

FIRST FLOOR

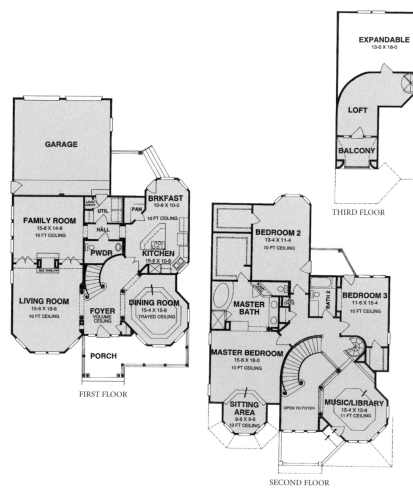

FIRST FLOOR

SECOND FLOOR

EXPANDABLE
13-0 X 18-0

LOFT

BALCONY

THIRD FLOOR

plan# HPK0700124

L

Design: HPK0700124
Style: Victorian
First Floor: 1,329 sq. ft.
Second Floor: 1,917 sq. ft.
Third Floor: 189 sq. ft.
Total: 3,435 sq. ft.
Bedrooms: 3
Bathrooms: 2½
Width: 40' - 4"
Depth: 62' - 0"
Foundation: Crawlspace

SEARCH ONLINE @ EPLANS.COM

While speaking clearly of the past, the inside of this Victorian home coincides with the open, flowing interiors of today. Dine in the elegant dining room with its tray ceiling, or move through the double French doors between the formal living room and informal family room to sense the livability of this charming home. The kitchen boasts a large pantry and a corner sink with a window. The lovely master suite resides upstairs. The raised sitting area off the master bedroom provides the owner with a mini-retreat for reading and relaxing. The second floor also includes two large bedrooms and a library/music room.

SECOND FLOOR

plan # HPK0700125

Style: Gothic Revival
First Floor: 2,023 sq. ft.
Second Floor: 749 sq. ft.
Total: 2,772 sq. ft.
Bonus Space: 242 sq. ft.
Bedrooms: 4
Bathrooms: 3½
Width: 77' - 2"
Depth: 57' - 11"
Foundation: Slab,
Unfinished Basement

SEARCH ONLINE @ EPLANS.COM

A wraparound porch makes this unique Victorian farmhouse stand out with style and grace, as does the lovely detailing of this plan. This design is versatile enough to accommodate either a small or large family. The entry is flanked on the left side by a large kitchen/breakfast area with an island, and on the right side by a parlor/music room. The family room is enhanced with a bar ledge, fireplace, and built-in entertainment center. The master suite has access to a covered deck. The upstairs level is shared by three bedrooms, two full baths, and a bonus room. A one-bedroom apartment is located over the garage.

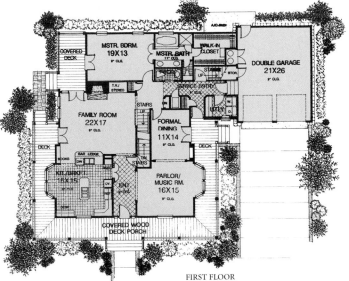

FIRST FLOOR

A Palladian window, fish-scale shingles, and turret-style bays set off this country-style Victorian exterior. An impressive tile entry opens to the formal rooms, which nestle to the left side of the plan. The turret houses a secluded study on the first floor and provides a sunny bay window for a family bedroom upstairs. The second-floor master suite features its own fireplace, a dressing area with a walk-in closet, and a lavish bath.

plan# HPK0700126

LD

Style: Victorian
First Floor: 1,186 sq. ft.
Second Floor: 988 sq. ft.
Total: 2,174 sq. ft.
Bedrooms: 4
Bathrooms: 2½
Width: 72' - 0"
Depth: 50' - 10"
Foundation: Unfinished Basement

SEARCH ONLINE @ EPLANS.COM

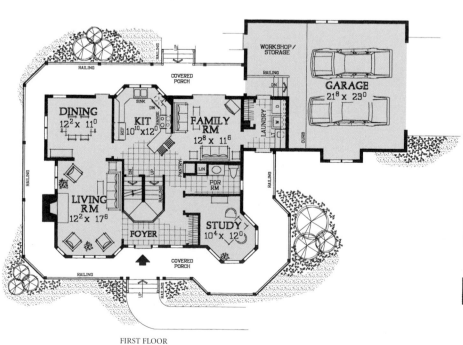

FIRST FLOOR

SECOND FLOOR

ORDER BLUEPRINTS 24 HOURS, 7 DAYS A WEEK, AT 1-800-521-6797

plan # HPK0700127

Style: Victorian
First Floor: 1,462 sq. ft.
Second Floor: 1,288 sq. ft.
Total: 2,750 sq. ft.
Bedrooms: 4
Bathrooms: 2½
Width: 70' - 8"
Depth: 54' - 0"
Foundation: Crawlspace,
Unfinished Basement

SEARCH ONLINE @ EPLANS.COM

A touch of Victoriana enhances the facade of this home: a turret roof over a wraparound porch with turned wood spindles. Special attractions on the first floor include a tray ceiling in the octagonal living room, fireplaces in the country kitchen and the living room, a coffered ceiling in the family room, and double-door access to the cozy den. The master suite boasts a coffered ceiling, walk-in closet, and whirlpool tub.

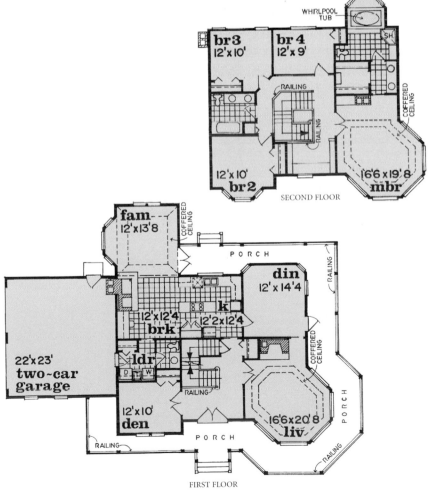

SECOND FLOOR

FIRST FLOOR

An interesting mixture of Victorian detailing and farmhouse convenience, this plan boasts a brick and siding exterior and decorative windows. The piece de resistance of this plan is the gracious porch that curves around the family room. The family room looks out through multipane windows to the front view. Opening to the patio, the living room features a sweeping sloped ceiling. The dining room and kitchen areas flow smoothly into one another, allowing for easy serving and conversation. Off the kitchen, steps lead to the basement below. The master bedroom, located upstairs, boasts a cathedral ceiling and a full bath with a skylight. Bedrooms 2 and 3 share a full bath on the second level as well.

plan# HPK0700128

Style: Farmhouse
First Floor: 1,157 sq. ft.
Second Floor: 838 sq. ft.
Total: 1,995 sq. ft.
Bedrooms: 3
Bathrooms: 2½
Width: 66' - 10"
Depth: 36' - 11"
Foundation: Crawlspace, Slab, Unfinished Basement

SEARCH ONLINE @ EPLANS.COM

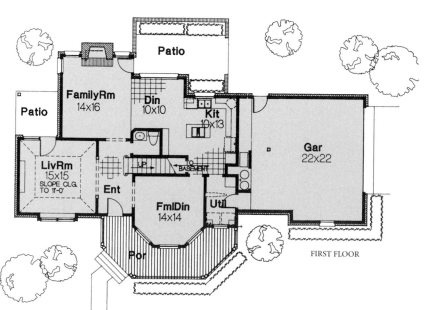

FIRST FLOOR

SECOND FLOOR

ORDER BLUEPRINTS 24 HOURS, 7 DAYS A WEEK, AT 1-800-521-6797

plan(#) HPK0700129

Style: Victorian
First Floor: 1,291 sq. ft.
Second Floor: 1,291 sq. ft.
Total: 2,582 sq. ft.
Bedrooms: 4
Bathrooms: 3
Width: 64' - 6"
Depth: 47' - 0"
Foundation: Crawlspace, Unfinished Basement

SEARCH ONLINE @ EPLANS.COM

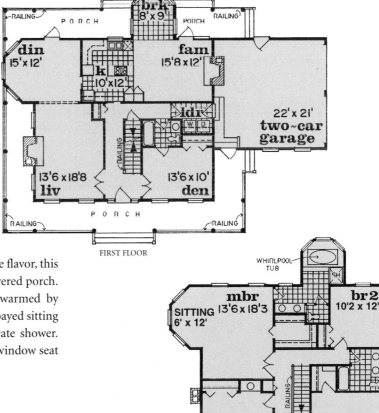

FIRST FLOOR

SECOND FLOOR

Traditional with an essence of farmhouse flavor, this four-bedroom home begins with a wraparound covered porch. Both the family room and the living room are warmed by hearths. The master suite on the second level has a bayed sitting room and a bath with a whirlpool tub and separate shower. Three family bedrooms share a full bath. Note the window seat on the second-floor landing.

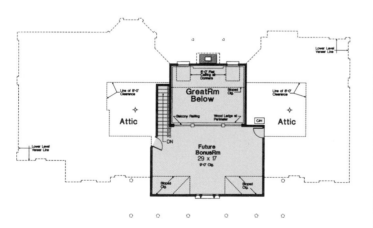

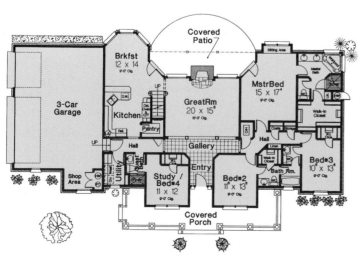

plan # HPK0700130

Style: Farmhouse
Square Footage: 2,293
Bonus Space: 536 sq. ft.
Bedrooms: 4
Bathrooms: 3
Width: 88' - 0"
Depth: 51' - 9"
Foundation: Slab,
Unfinished Basement

SEARCH ONLINE @ EPLANS.COM

Special gatherings and events will take place in the heart of this splendid home. The great room, defined by columns, includes a hearth and views to the covered patio. The east wing is occupied by the sleeping quarters, with a master bedroom which features an exclusive master bath. Two family bedrooms both have walk-in closets and share a compartmented bath with twin vanities. The three-car garage opens to the hall where the utility room, the kitchen, and an additional bedroom/study can be accessed. A future bonus room is also available upstairs.

ORDER BLUEPRINTS 24 HOURS, 7 DAYS A WEEK, AT 1-800-521-6797

plan # HPK0700131

Style: Victorian
First Floor: 1,320 sq. ft.
Second Floor: 1,268 sq. ft.
Total: 2,588 sq. ft.
Bonus Space: 389 sq. ft.
Bedrooms: 4
Bathrooms: 2½
Width: 45' - 0"
Depth: 64' - 0"
Foundation: Slab,
Unfinished Basement

SEARCH ONLINE @ EPLANS.COM

Country farmhouse with a touch of Victorian gingerbread describes this two-story design. Formal elegance unfolds as you enter the foyer, flanked by living and dining rooms. Three bedrooms share a hall bath while the master enjoys pampering amenities: garden tub, adjoining shower, double sinks, a dressing vanity, and an oversized walk-in closet. The family room features a full window wall that overlooks the deck.

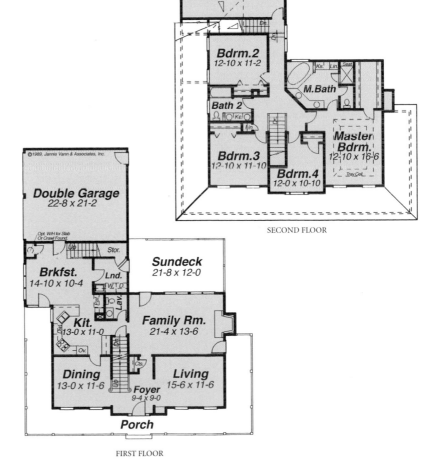

SECOND FLOOR

FIRST FLOOR

Covered porches both front and back extend the living spaces to the outdoors. The foyer opens to the great room, with its coffered ceiling and twin French doors, and the dining room on the right. The angled kitchen is nestled between the dining room and the breakfast bay serving both with ease and efficiency. The lavish master suite resides on the right for privacy while the two additional bedrooms are situated on the left.

plan# HPK0700132

Style: Victorian
Square Footage: 1,989
Bonus Space: 274 sq. ft.
Bedrooms: 3
Bathrooms: 2
Width: 81' - 0"
Depth: 50' - 0"
Foundation: Crawlspace

SEARCH ONLINE @ EPLANS.COM

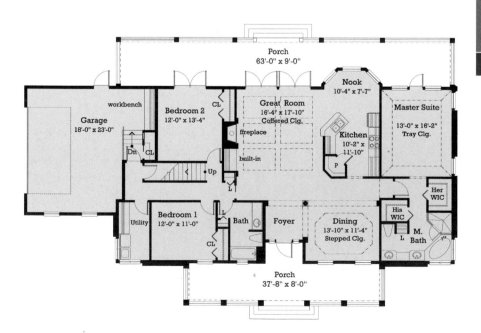

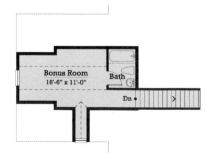

© Copyright 2003, Garrell Associates, Inc.

plan# HPK0700133

Style: Victorian
First Floor: 1,649 sq. ft.
Second Floor: 1,604 sq. ft.
Total: 3,253 sq. ft.
Bedrooms: 4
Bathrooms: 3½
Width: 54' - 0"
Depth: 45' - 8"
Foundation: Slab, Unfinished Walkout Basement

SEARCH ONLINE @ EPLANS.COM

Coastal living at its finest, this home wears cedar shingles and siding with perfection. Front and rear porches extend living space for the family that loves the outdoors. Entertain on the weekend with well-designed formal spaces that flank the foyer. An open gallery hall transitions to the relaxed grand room featuring a fireplace and a wall of windows. Stairs to the second floor are to the rear. A spacious breakfast room offers lounging opportunity for guests to keep the cook company in the nearby fantastic island kitchen. Upstairs, large bedrooms give the family plenty of elbow room. A study loft is a great place for homework and an internet connection. Framed by double doors, the master suite thinks of everything. A private bath features dual-sink vanity, separate tub and shower, compartmented toilet, and oversized walk-in closet.

FIRST FLOOR

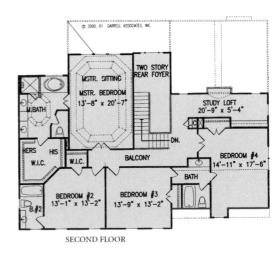

SECOND FLOOR

Special exterior details—a railed veranda, multipane windows, and a dormer—lend a country flavor to this three-bedroom home. A central hall at the entry holds a half-bath and a stair to the second floor and also allows passage to the formal living and dining rooms. The living room has a fireplace; the dining room features a private veranda. The country kitchen also has a fireplace and opens to a patio with a built-in barbecue.

plan # HPK0700134

Style: Victorian
First Floor: 879 sq. ft.
Second Floor: 869 sq. ft.
Total: 1,748 sq. ft.
Bedrooms: 3
Bathrooms: 2½
Width: 37' - 6"
Depth: 47' - 10"
Foundation: Crawlspace, Unfinished Basement

SEARCH ONLINE @ EPLANS.COM

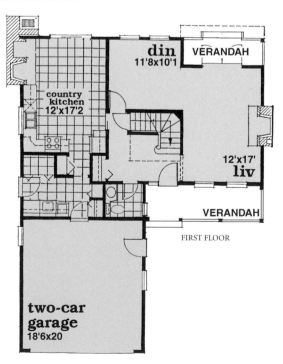

FIRST FLOOR

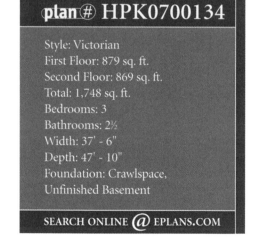

SECOND FLOOR

plan# HPK0700135

Style: Victorian
First Floor: 1,653 sq. ft.
Second Floor: 700 sq. ft.
Total: 2,353 sq. ft.
Bedrooms: 4
Bathrooms: 2½
Width: 54' - 0"
Depth: 50' - 0"

SEARCH ONLINE @ EPLANS.COM

Beautiful arches and elaborate detail give the elevation of this four-bedroom home an unmistakable elegance. The formal dining room with a bay window is visible from the entrance hall. A large great room has a through-fireplace and a wall of windows. A hearth room adjoins the kitchen area. On the first floor, the master suite features His and Hers wardrobes, a large whirlpool tub, and two vanities. Upstairs, family sleeping quarters share a full compartmented bath.

QUOTE ONE®

SECOND FLOOR

FIRST FLOOR

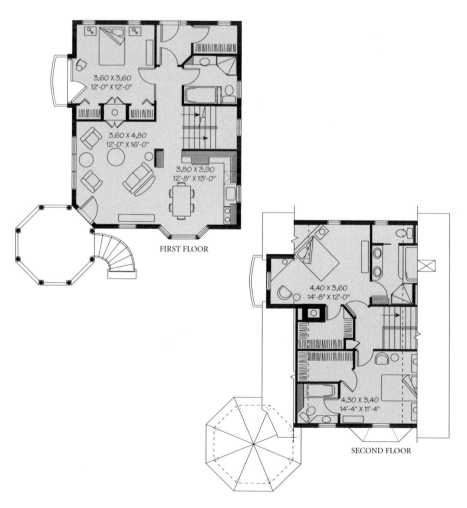

FIRST FLOOR

3,60 X 3,60
12'-0" X 12'-0"

3,60 X 4,80
12'-0" X 16'-0"

3,80 X 3,90
12'-8" X 13'-0"

SECOND FLOOR

4,40 X 3,60
14'-8" X 12'-0"

4,30 X 3,40
14'-4" X 11'-4"

plan# HPK0700136

Style: Victorian
First Floor: 840 sq. ft.
Second Floor: 757 sq. ft.
Total: 1,597 sq. ft.
Bedrooms: 3
Bathrooms: 3
Width: 26' - 0"
Depth: 32' - 0"
Foundation: Unfinished Basement

SEARCH ONLINE @ EPLANS.COM

The amazing turret/gazebo porch on this classy home has an authentic Victorian flavor. The bedroom on the first level offers a protruding balcony. The entrance leads to the living room, located just left of the dining area and L-shaped kitchen. The master suite features a private bath with dual sinks. Two more family bedrooms are located on the second level.

ORDER BLUEPRINTS 24 HOURS, 7 DAYS A WEEK, AT 1-800-521-6797

plan# HPK0700137

Style: Victorian
Square Footage: 1,466
Bedrooms: 3
Bathrooms: 2
Width: 60' - 0"
Depth: 39' - 10"
Foundation: Unfinished Basement, Slab, Crawlspace

SEARCH ONLINE @ EPLANS.COM

This absolutely charming Victorian-style ranch home is warm and inviting, yet the interior is decidedly up-to-date. An assemblage of beautiful windows surrounds the main entry, flooding the entrance foyer and adjoining great room with an abundance of shaded light. An elegant 10-foot stepped ceiling is featured in the great room, as is a corner fireplace and rear wall of French-style sliding doors. The beautiful multisided breakfast room features a 16-foot ceiling adorned with high clerestory windows, which become the exterior "turret." A private master suite includes a compartmented bath, dressing alcove, very large walk-in closet, 10-foot stepped ceiling, and beautiful bay window overlooking the rear.

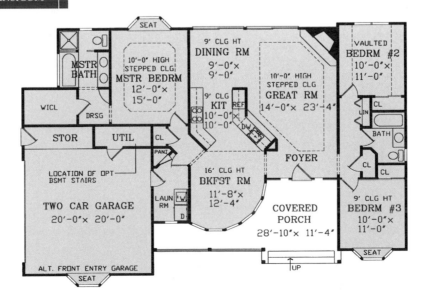

SECOND FLOOR

FIRST FLOOR

plan # HPK0700138

Style: Victorian
First Floor: 1,337 sq. ft.
Second Floor: 1,025 sq. ft.
Total: 2,362 sq. ft.
Bedrooms: 3
Bathrooms: 2½
Width: 47' - 0"
Depth: 72' - 6"
Foundation: Unfinished
Basement, Crawlspace

SEARCH ONLINE @ EPLANS.COM

Victorian elegance enhances this day-dreamer design. A beautiful wraparound porch lends a cozy addition, which enlarges the appearance of the exterior facade. Enter through the foyer into a combined living room/dining area to the right. An efficient island kitchen at the rear of the plan sits opposite the breakfast nook and conveniently accesses the two-car garage. The family room includes a warming fireplace. A gazebo-style den offers quiet seclusion and completes the first floor. Winding upstairs, the master suite includes a vaulted ceiling, a spacious private bath, and a walk-in closet. Two additional bedrooms share a hall bath.

ORDER BLUEPRINTS 24 HOURS, 7 DAYS A WEEK, AT 1-800-521-6797

plan # HPK0700139

Style: Victorian
First Floor: 1,081 sq. ft.
Second Floor: 1,136 sq. ft.
Total: 2,217 sq. ft.
Bedrooms: 4
Bathrooms: 2½
Width: 53' - 0"
Depth: 42' - 0"

SEARCH ONLINE @ EPLANS.COM

Victorian charm and detailing radiate from this design. Inside, formal living spaces begin with a dining room with hutch space and a parlor highlighted by a bayed window. The T-shaped staircase allows quick access to the informal spaces at the rear, such as the comfortable gathering room with a fireplace, built-in bookcase, and many windows. Upstairs, a compartmented bath is shared by the secondary sleeping quarters. Gracing the master sleeping quarters is a private dressing/bath area offering an oval whirlpool tub, angled vanity and walk-in wardrobe.

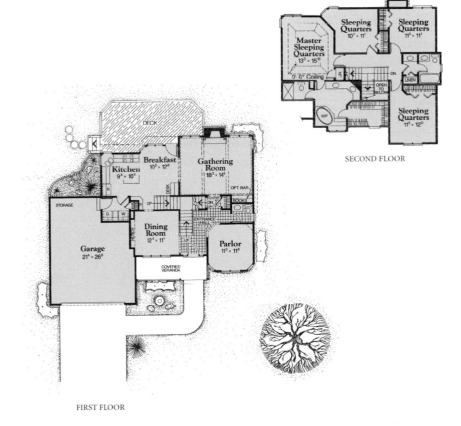

SECOND FLOOR

FIRST FLOOR

FIRST FLOOR

DECK
30'-6" x 11'-7"

BRKFST

KITCHEN
15'-0" x 17'-0"

DINING
14'-8" x 12'-8"

FAMILY
18'-8" x 16'-0"

ENTRY
7'-11" x 15'-6"

UP

COATS

PORCH
30'-6" x 7'-7"

TRAY CEILING

MASTER BDRM
16'-4" x 15'-0"

D   W

DN

BEDROOM 2
12'-0" x 12'-8"

BEDROOM 3
12'-8" x 12'-0"

WINDOW SEAT

SECOND FLOOR

plan# HPK0700140

Style: Victorian
First Floor: 1,009 sq. ft.
Second Floor: 976 sq. ft.
Total: 1,985 sq. ft.
Bedrooms: 3
Bathrooms: 2½
Width: 31' - 2"
Depth: 42' - 0"
Foundation: Unfinished Walkout
Basement, Crawlspace

SEARCH ONLINE @ EPLANS.COM

Fine details accentuate the heirloom doll-house beauty of this narrow-lot Victorian home. Plenty of living space for get togethers and scaled just right for solitary evenings, the dining room's twin set of French doors can be kept open to expand the footprint or shut off when not in use. An eat-in island kitchen makes room for casual meals and offers access to the rear deck. French doors also enhance the family room and provide front porch access. Two secondary bedrooms share a compartmented bath and enjoy unique windows. The master suite is dressed up with a tray ceiling, French door access to the roomy bath, and a walk-in closet.

OLD-WORLD INSPIRATION

All American homes have their roots in the styles of Europe that the first colonists brought with them. While Colonial, Craftsman, and Bungalow homes all borrowed from these European themes, other American homes reflected a more literal interpretation of Old World design.

These styles remain popular today, especially in the country. Traveling America's back roads, you can often stumble upon a home that would look just as comfortable in the French countryside.

These homes typically have a stone facade, or something similar, since European homes relied much less on wood than those in Colonial America. The effect can pro-duce a home that's just as rustic as a country cottage or Craftsman design.

That use of stone can echo the natural surroundings of a country home, and demonstrates the appreciation of the outdoors. That can be seen further in the incorporation of porches, decks, and patios in these homes, along with the use of large windows to showcase the outdoor space and emphasize nature. ■

Simple lines and a stucco facade lend a European flavor to this country cottage. For more details on Design HPK0700161, see page 174.

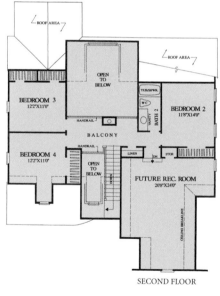

SECOND FLOOR

FIRST FLOOR

plan# HPK0700141

Style: European Cottage
First Floor: 1,627 sq. ft.
Second Floor: 783 sq. ft.
Total: 2,410 sq. ft.
Bonus Space: 418 sq. ft.
Bedrooms: 4
Bathrooms: 2½
Width: 46' - 0"
Depth: 58' - 6"
Foundation: Crawlspace

SEARCH ONLINE @ EPLANS.COM

This "little jewel" of a home emanates a warmth and joy not soon forgotten. The two-story foyer leads to the formal living room, defined by graceful columns. A formal dining room opens off from the living room, making entertaining a breeze. A family room at the back features a fireplace and works well with the kitchen and breakfast areas. A lavish master suite is secluded on the first floor; three family bedrooms reside upstairs.

© 2001 Donald A. Gardner, Inc.

plan# HPK0700142

Style: European Cottage
First Floor: 1,547 sq. ft.
Second Floor: 684 sq. ft.
Total: 2,231 sq. ft.
Bonus Space: 300 sq. ft.
Bedrooms: 3
Bathrooms: 2½
Width: 59' - 2"
Depth: 44' - 4"

SEARCH ONLINE @ EPLANS.COM

Stone and siding create a stunning exterior, especially when combined with a sloped roofline and a decorative wood bracket. A metal roof embellishes the garage's box-bay window, and arches are seen in and above windows as well as the front entrance. The great room is filled with light from its many windows and French doors, and a glimpse of the fireplace can be seen from every gathering room. The master bedroom is topped by a cathedral ceiling and has a large walk-in closet. The loft makes a perfect sitting or study area that receives a lot of light from the open, two-story great room. The second floor bathroom includes twin lavatories, and the versatile bonus room is easily accessible.

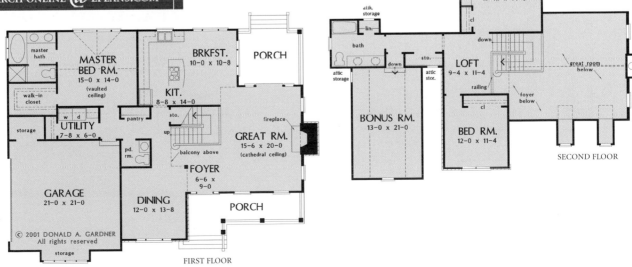

FIRST FLOOR

SECOND FLOOR

Multipane windows, shutters, and shingle accents adorn the stucco facade of this wonderful French Country home. Inside, the foyer introduces the hearth-warmed great room that features French-door access to the rear deck. The dining room, defined from the foyer and great room by columns, enjoys front-yard views. The master bedroom includes two walk-in closets, rear-deck access, and a dual vanity bath.

plan# HPK0700143

Style: European Cottage
First Floor: 1,840 sq. ft.
Second Floor: 840 sq. ft.
Total: 2,680 sq. ft.
Bonus Space: 295 sq. ft.
Bedrooms: 3
Bathrooms: 2½
Width: 66' - 0"
Depth: 65' - 10"
Foundation: Crawlspace

SEARCH ONLINE @ EPLANS.COM

Two Car Garage 23⁰ x 23⁰

Deck

Kitchen 11⁰ x 11⁰

Great Room 20⁶ x 21⁶

Master Bedroom 18³ x 14³

Breakfast 15³ x 7⁹

Family Room 15³ x 9⁶

Dining Room 14⁹ x 13³

FIRST FLOOR

Bedroom #2 13³ x 14³

Unfinished Bedroom 11³ x 15³

Bedroom #3 12⁰ x 15⁶

Study 8⁶ x 9⁹

SECOND FLOOR

REAR EXTERIOR

ORDER BLUEPRINTS 24 HOURS, 7 DAYS A WEEK, AT 1-800-521-6797

plan # HPK0700144

Style: European Cottage
Square Footage: 1,810
Bedrooms: 3
Bathrooms: 2
Width: 67' - 8"
Depth: 45' - 0"
Foundation: Unfinished Basement

SEARCH ONLINE @ EPLANS.COM

French Country rural style sets the tone for this pleasing one-story home. Stucco and stone create a vibrant and eye-catching facade and an open, flexible floor plan works for a modern family or empty-nester. Two family bedrooms are easily converted into a guest room and home office. A full hall bath is nearby. A formal dining room is perfect for dinner parties and holidays without being cut off from the rest of the home. A surprisingly versatile kitchen sports an island, great counter space, and adjoining eating nook. Flowing right into the living room, the kitchen works as a complementary space.

© Stephen Fuller, Inc.

plan# HPK0700145

Style: European Cottage
Square Footage: 2,494
Bedrooms: 3
Bathrooms: 2½
Width: 65' - 4"
Depth: 61' - 8"
Foundation: Finished
Walkout Basement

SEARCH ONLINE @ EPLANS.COM

Stucco and stone, multipane windows, a covered porch—all elements of a fine European-flavored home. Inside, the foyer is flanked by formal living and dining rooms and leads back to more casual areas. Here, a great room with a warming fireplace is framed by windows, with a nearby kitchen and breakfast room finishing off gathering areas. Two family bedrooms reside to the right and share a full bath that includes two vanities. The master suite is sure to please with a large walk-in closet and a sumptuous master bath.

plan # HPK0700146

Style: European Cottage
Square Footage: 2,170
Bedrooms: 4
Bathrooms: 3
Width: 62' - 0"
Depth: 61' - 6"
Foundation: Finished
Walkout Basement

SEARCH ONLINE @ EPLANS.COM

This classic cottage boasts a stone-and-wood exterior with a welcoming arch-top entry. An extended-hearth fireplace is the focal point of the family room, and a nearby sunroom opens up the living area to the outdoors. Sleeping quarters include a master wing with a spacious, angled bath and a sitting room or den that has its own full bath. On the opposite side of the plan, two family bedrooms share a full bath.

REAR EXTERIOR

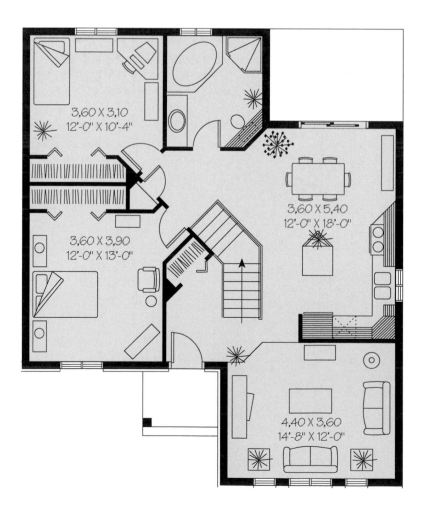

3,60 X 3,10
12'-0" X 10'-4"

3,60 X 3,90
12'-0" X 13'-0"

3,60 X 5,40
12'-0" X 18'-0"

4,40 X 3,60
14'-8" X 12'-0"

plan # HPK0700147

Style: European Cottage
Square Footage: 1,087
Bedrooms: 2
Bathrooms: 1
Width: 34' - 0"
Depth: 40' - 0"
Foundation: Unfinished Basement

SEARCH ONLINE @ EPLANS.COM

This one-story cottage, inspired by European architecture, is perfect as a vacation retreat, for empty-nesters, or for a family just starting out. An L-shaped kitchen and attached dining area are open to each other, and close enough to the family room to achieve true ease of serving. Two bedrooms and a full bath complete this plan.

plan# HPK0700148

Style: European Cottage
Square Footage: 2,322
Bedrooms: 4
Bathrooms: 2½
Width: 68' - 11"
Depth: 74' - 0"
Foundation: Slab

SEARCH ONLINE @ EPLANS.COM

A stucco-and-brick facade declares the Old World influence in this design. The steeply pitched roofline adds airiness to the interior spaces. The central entry opens to living spaces: a dining room on the left and the family room with a fireplace on the right. The kitchen and breakfast nook are nearby. The kitchen features an island cooktop and a huge pantry. A door in the breakfast room leads out to the rear porch. The bedrooms include three family bedrooms—one of which could be used as a study—and a master suite. Note the double closets in the master bath.

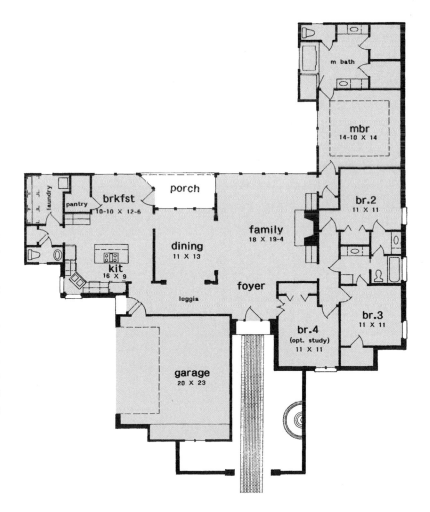

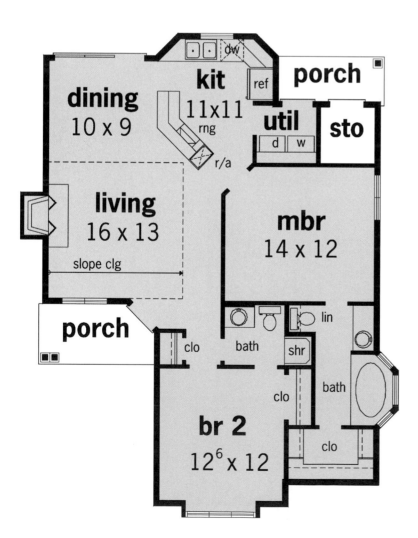

dining
10 x 9

kit
11x11
rng

porch

ref

util
d w

sto

living
16 x 13

slope clg

mbr
14 x 12

porch

clo

bath

shr

lin

clo

bath

clo

br 2
12⁶ x 12

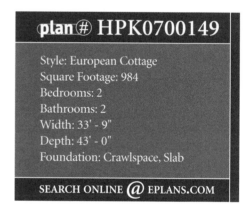

plan# HPK0700149

Style: European Cottage
Square Footage: 984
Bedrooms: 2
Bathrooms: 2
Width: 33' - 9"
Depth: 43' - 0"
Foundation: Crawlspace, Slab

SEARCH ONLINE @ EPLANS.COM

This snug home uses space efficiently, with no wasted square feet. Brightened by a clerestory window, the living room features a sloped ceiling and a warming fireplace. A spacious master suite enjoys a walk-in closet and a lavish bath with a garden tub set in a bay. The secondary bedroom has access to the hall bath. Wood trim and eye-catching windows make this home charming as well as practical.

A multitude of windows welcomes in the warm summer breezes in this delightful two-story stucco home. The den/living room off the foyer offers privacy with French-door access. The great room adds elegance with columns and arches as well as a majestic fireplace. The master suite boasts a private bath and view of the backyard.

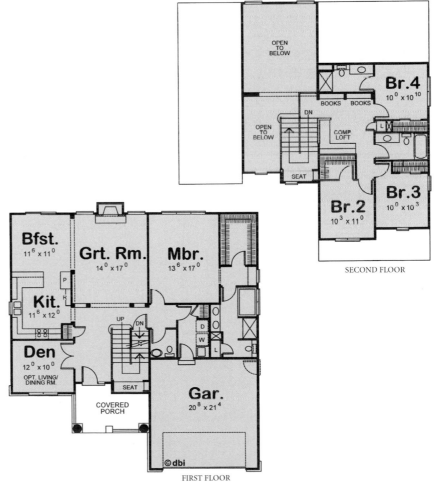

SECOND FLOOR

FIRST FLOOR

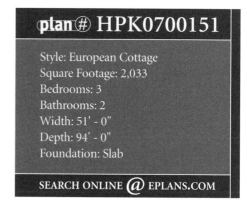

plan# HPK0700151

Style: European Cottage
Square Footage: 2,033
Bedrooms: 3
Bathrooms: 2
Width: 51' - 0"
Depth: 94' - 0"
Foundation: Slab

SEARCH ONLINE @ EPLANS.COM

A beautiful wraparound porch with columns and two dormers set above welcomes guests inside from the courtyard entry. The foyer introduces the formal dining area to the right, near the island kitchen and breakfast nook. A fireplace warms the living room, while plenty of windows draw in natural light. The master suite sits at the rear of the plan and features a plush bath with two walk-in closets. Two family bedrooms share a dual-vanity bath.

plan# HPK0700152

Style: European Cottage
Square Footage: 1,760
Bedrooms: 3
Bathrooms: 2
Width: 42' - 6"
Depth: 56' - 11"
Foundation: Slab

SEARCH ONLINE @ EPLANS.COM

French influences preside upon the facade of this enchanting cottage that enjoys and abundance of windows in the rear. The two family bedrooms to the left of the entry enjoy a conveniently placed full bath. The foyer leads to the family room at the rear with its window wall and fireplace flanked by built-ins. The island kitchen offers a pantry and plenty of counter space. The master suite is on the right with a lavish private bath.

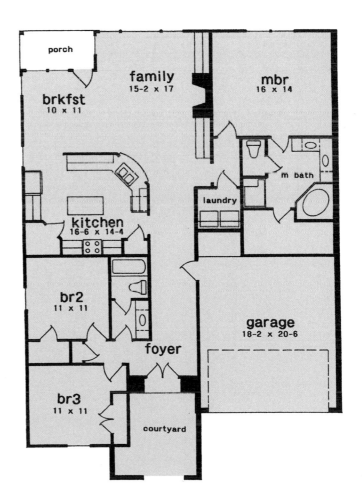

13'-8" X 21'-4"
4,10 X 6,40

8'-4" X 11'-4"
2,50 X 3,40

9'-8" X 13'-0"
2,90 X 3,90

10'-0" X 10'-0"
3,00 X 3,00

12'-0" X 15'-0"
3,60 X 4,50

11'-0" X 13'-0"
3,30 X 3,90

plan# HPK0700153

Style: European Cottage
Square Footage: 1,072
Bedrooms: 2
Bathrooms: 1
Width: 32' - 0"
Depth: 42' - 0"
Foundation: Unfinished Basement

SEARCH ONLINE @ EPLANS.COM

Gentle arches separating front-porch columns and hipped rooflines distinguish this handsome one-story home, perfect for a new family. From the warming fireplace in the front living room to the open space of the combined kitchen and dining area, this plan promises both comfort and convenience. The master bedroom, which enjoys a walk-in wardrobe, shares a splendid bath with a second bedroom. It includes a walk-in shower, but winning marks go to the magnificent corner garden tub. A rear deck and unattached garage complete this plan.

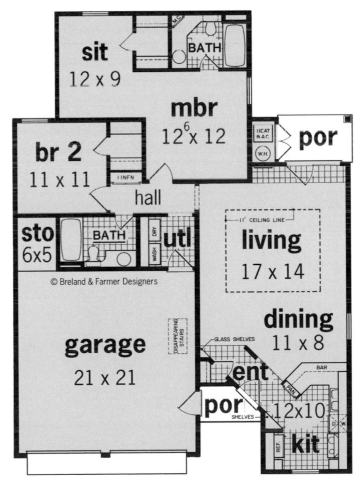

plan# HPK0700154

Style: European Cottage
Square Footage: 1,150
Bedrooms: 2
Bathrooms: 2
Width: 38' - 0"
Depth: 52' - 0"
Foundation: Slab, Crawlspace

SEARCH ONLINE @ EPLANS.COM

A hipped roof and interesting angles give this compact home its charm. Inside, the entry leads to a galley kitchen with a breakfast bar. A dining/living room creates a feeling of spaciousness. The living room has a raised ceiling and opens to the backyard. The master suite is complete with a private bath and a sitting room for quiet contemplation.

© 2000 Donald A. Gardner, Inc.

This elegant design brings back the sophistication and elegance of days gone by, yet its modern layout creates a natural traffic flow to enhance easy living. Columns partition space without enclosing it, while built-ins in the great room and counter space in the utility/mud room add convenience. The family-efficient floor plan can be witnessed in the kitchen's handy pass-through, and the kitchen has access to the rear porch for outdoor entertaining. Cathedral ceilings highlight the master bedroom and bedroom/study, while vaulted ceilings top the breakfast area and loft/study. The bonus room can be used as a home theater, playroom, or gym, and its position allows it to keep recreational noise away from the house proper.

plan# HPK0700155

Style: European Cottage
First Floor: 2,477 sq. ft.
Second Floor: 742 sq. ft.
Total: 3,219 sq. ft.
Bonus Space: 419 sq. ft.
Bedrooms: 4
Bathrooms: 4
Width: 99' - 10"
Depth: 66' - 2"

SEARCH ONLINE @ EPLANS.COM

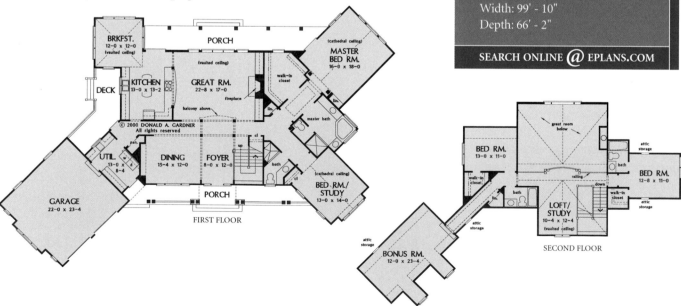

J.N. HANSEN S.D.G.

plan# HPK0700156

Style: European Cottage
Square Footage: 2,816
Bonus Space: 290 sq. ft.
Bedrooms: 4
Bathrooms: 3½ + ½
Width: 94' - 0"
Depth: 70' - 5"
Foundation: Slab

SEARCH ONLINE @ EPLANS.COM

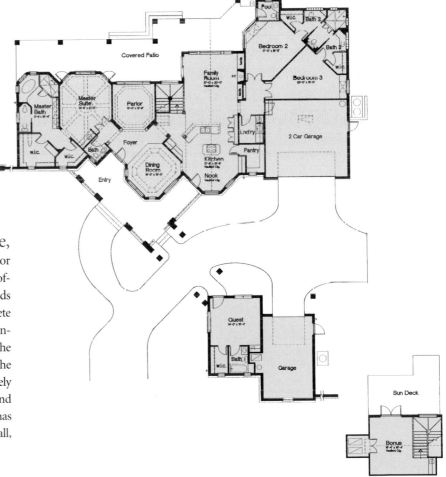

Though designed as a grand estate, this home retains the warmth of a country manor with intimate details, on the inside and out. A one-of-a-kind drive court leads to private parking and ends in a two-car garage; a separate guest house is replete with angled walls and sculptured ceilings. A continuous vault follows from the family room through the kitchen and nook. The vault soars even higher in the bonus room with a sundeck upstairs. Two exquisitely appointed family bedrooms with window seats and walk-in closets share a full bath. The master suite has pampering details such as a juice bar and media wall, walk-in closets, and covered patio access.

REAR EXTERIOR

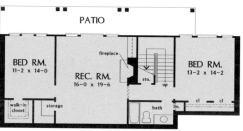

MAIN LEVEL

LOWER LEVEL

© 1999 DONALD A. GARDNER
All rights reserved

The vaulted foyer receives light from two clerestory dormer windows and includes a niche for displaying collectibles. The generous great room enjoys a dramatic cathedral ceiling, a fireplace, and built-in bookshelves. A recreation room is located on the basement level. Two bedrooms can be found on the main floor, while two more flank the rec room downstairs. The master suite boasts an elegant tray ceiling and a luxurious bath.

plan# HPK0700158

Style: European Cottage
Square Footage: 2,140
Bedrooms: 4
Bathrooms: 3
Width: 62' - 0"
Depth: 60' - 6"
Foundation: Finished
Walkout Basement

SEARCH ONLINE @ EPLANS.COM

Imagine the luxurious living you'll enjoy in this beautiful home! The natural beauty of stone combined with sophisticated window detailing represents the good taste you'll find carried throughout the design. Common living areas include the great room with a fireplace, the sun room, and the breakfast area, plus rear and side porches. The master suite features private access to the rear porch and a wonderfully planned bath.

With a delightful flavor, this two-story home features family living at its best. The foyer opens to a study or living room on the left. The dining room on the right offers large proportions and full windows. The family room remains open to the kitchen and the breakfast room. Here, sunny meals are guaranteed with a bay window overlooking the rear yard. In the master suite, a bayed sitting area, a walk-in closet, and a pampering bath are sure to please. Upstairs, two family bedrooms flank a loft or study area.

plan # HPK0700159

Style: European Cottage
First Floor: 1,715 sq. ft.
Second Floor: 620 sq. ft.
Total: 2,335 sq. ft.
Bonus Space: 265 sq. ft.
Bedrooms: 3
Bathrooms: 2½
Width: 58' - 6"
Depth: 50' - 3"

SEARCH ONLINE @ EPLANS.COM

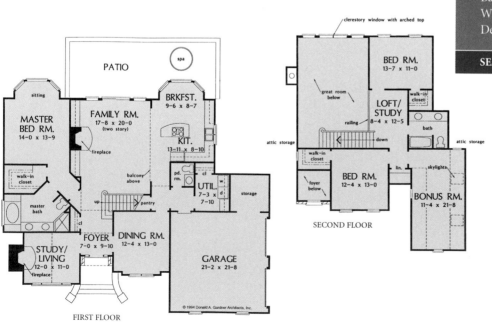

FIRST FLOOR

SECOND FLOOR

ORDER BLUEPRINTS 24 HOURS, 7 DAYS A WEEK, AT 1-800-521-6797

plan # HPK0700160

Style: European Cottage
First Floor: 1,918 sq. ft.
Second Floor: 469 sq. ft.
Total: 2,387 sq. ft.
Bonus Space: 374 sq. ft.
Bedrooms: 4
Bathrooms: 3
Width: 73' - 3"
Depth: 43' - 6"

SEARCH ONLINE @ EPLANS.COM

Enjoy the elegance of the stone-and-stucco exterior on this amenity-filled four-bedroom home. An impressive fireplace features built-ins to each side within the great room. The secondary bedroom on the first floor—or make it a study—provides access to a full bath. The tray-ceilinged master suite includes a sumptuous bath, two walk-in closets, and a bay window. Two secondary bedrooms, a bonus room, and a full bath reside on the second floor.

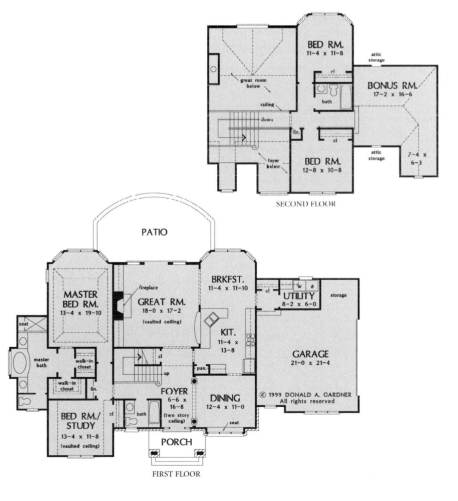

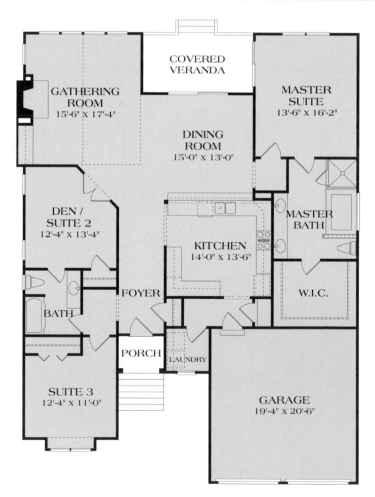

plan# HPK0700161

Style: European Cottage
Square Footage: 1,915
Bedrooms: 3
Bathrooms: 2
Width: 46' - 0"
Depth: 60' - 2"
Foundation: Crawlspace

SEARCH ONLINE @ EPLANS.COM

A sunny box-bay window and a shady recessed entry create an elegant impression in this lovely design. The sleeping quarters are arranged for privacy along the perimeter of the spacious living areas. The kitchen provides a generous work space, and the dining room is open to the gathering room with its fireplace. To the rear, a covered veranda is accessible from the dining room and the master suite. Note the lavish bath and huge walk-in closet in the master suite.

ORDER BLUEPRINTS 24 HOURS, 7 DAYS A WEEK, AT 1-800-521-6797

plan# HPK0700162

Style: French Cottage
First Floor: 2,384 sq. ft.
Second Floor: 1,050 sq. ft.
Total: 3,434 sq. ft.
Bonus Space: 228 sq. ft.
Bedrooms: 4
Bathrooms: 3½
Width: 63' - 4"
Depth: 57' - 0"
Foundation: Crawlspace,
Unfinished Walkout Basement

SEARCH ONLINE @ EPLANS.COM

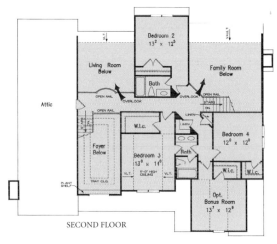

SECOND FLOOR

The covered front porch of this stucco home opens to a two-story foyer and one of two staircases. Arched openings lead into both the formal dining room and the vaulted living room. The efficient kitchen features a walk-in pantry, built-in desk, work island, and separate snack bar. Nearby, the large breakfast area opens to the family room. Lavish in its amenities, the master suite offers a separate vaulted sitting room with a fireplace, among other luxuries. Three bedrooms, along with optional bonus space and attic storage, are found on the second floor.

FIRST FLOOR

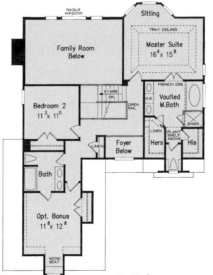

SECOND FLOOR

Sitting

RADIUS WINDOW

Family Room Below

TRAY CEILING

Master Suite
16⁶ x 15⁸

STAIRS DN.

Vaulted M.Bath

FRENCH DRS.

OPEN RAIL

K.S.

Bedroom 2
11³ x 11⁰

LINEN

PLANT SHELF ABOVE

SHWR.

Foyer Below

Hers

His

LINEN

Bath

Opt. Bonus
11⁸ x 12⁸

WDW SEAT

plan # HPK0700163

Style: European Cottage
First Floor: 1,191 sq. ft.
Second Floor: 824 sq. ft.
Total: 2,015 sq. ft.
Bonus Space: 199 sq. ft.
Bedrooms: 3
Bathrooms: 3
Width: 41' - 6"
Depth: 55' - 0"
Foundation: Crawlspace,
Unfinished Walkout Basement

SEARCH ONLINE @ EPLANS.COM

With a stucco facade and stone accents, this gorgeous French-influenced cottage will look great in any neighborhood. A side-loading garage makes this home perfect for a corner lot—the dormer window above holds a window seat in the bonus room. Inside, the grand foyer opens to the right to an elegant dining room with a box-bay window. Ahead, an open kitchen flows into the bayed breakfast nook with ease. Radius windows brighten the two-story family room, welcoming with a warming fireplace. An adjacent bedroom/study makes a perfect guest room or home office. Upstairs, a bedroom shares a bath with the bonus room (or make it another bedroom). The master suite is a lovely retreat, with a bayed sitting area, French doors, a vaulted bath, and His and Hers walk-in closets.

FRENCH DOOR

Breakfast

Laund.

Two Story Family Room
20⁰ x 13⁵

FPL

SERVING BAR

RANGE

Kitchen

DW.

PANT.

REF.

STAIRS DN.

Bedroom 3/ Study
11³ x 11⁰

STAIRS UP

OPEN RAIL

COATS

Two Story Foyer

Dining Room
12² x 13⁹

W.i.c.

Bath

COVERED ENTRY

Garage
20⁵ x 21⁰

FIRST FLOOR

plan # HPK0700164

Style: European Cottage
Square Footage: 2,713
Bonus Space: 440 sq. ft.
Bedrooms: 3
Bathrooms: 3
Width: 66' - 4"
Depth: 80' - 8"
Foundation: Slab

SEARCH ONLINE @ EPLANS.COM

Interesting arches, columns, and cantilevers adorn this shingled home. A large living room enjoys rear views and the covered porch. The island kitchen has an abundance of counter space and directly flows into a bayed breakfast nook. The hearth-warmed family room boasts easy access to the kitchen. The master bedroom resides on the right side of the plan; amenities include His and Hers walk-in closets and sinks, a garden tub, separate shower, compartmented toilet, and a sitting bay that looks to the rear porch.

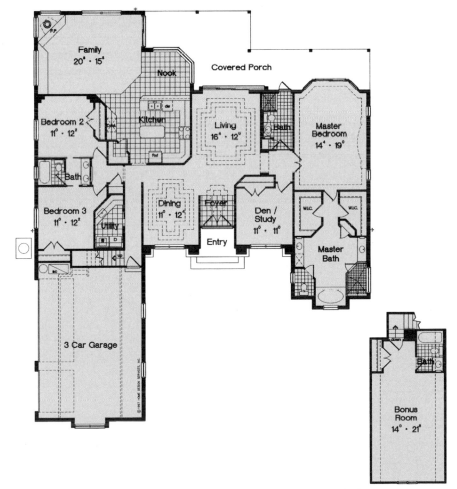

English and French influences create dramatic rooflines and this home's perfect proportions are highlighted by cedar shingles and stonework. A lovely embellished entry porch bespeaks the rich amenities and functionality of this floor plan. French doors open to the den or formal dining room. Three beautiful windows add sublime natural light and give an expansive feeling to the great room. Built-ins and a see-through fireplace divide the great room from the modern hearth room, eating nook, and kitchen combination. Privacy is king in the master suite. More French doors enhance the bathroom featuring dual sinks, separate shower and tub, and a walk-in closet. Upstairs, three family bedrooms share a full hall bath.

plan# HPK0700165

Style: European Cottage
First Floor: 1,754 sq. ft.
Second Floor: 744 sq. ft.
Total: 2,498 sq. ft.
Bedrooms: 4
Bathrooms: 2½
Width: 69' - 0"
Depth: 52' - 8"
Foundation: Unfinished Basement

SEARCH ONLINE @ EPLANS.COM

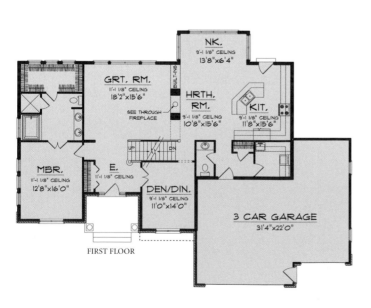

FIRST FLOOR

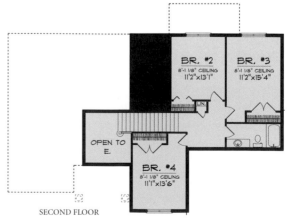

SECOND FLOOR

plan# HPK0700166

Style: European Cottage
First Floor: 1,730 sq. ft.
Second Floor: 1,223 sq. ft.
Total: 2,953 sq. ft.
Bedrooms: 3
Bathrooms: 3
Width: 66' - 0"
Depth: 49' - 0"
Foundation: Slab

SEARCH ONLINE @ EPLANS.COM

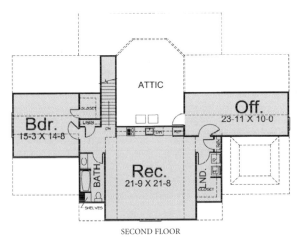

SECOND FLOOR

Gorgeous stone and siding make up the facade of this symmetrically fashioned home. Enter into the foyer, flanked on the left by a flexible study or guest room and on the right by the dining room. Straight ahead is family room with coffered ceiling, with access to an expansive rear porch. To the right of the family room are the kitchen and adjacent breakfast nook. The master suite and bath, with a separate shower and tub, and a large walk-in closet, complete the first level. Upstairs you'll find a laundry room, a third bedroom and full bath, and a convenient home office.

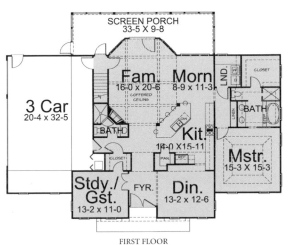

FIRST FLOOR

plan# **HPK0700167**

Style: European Cottage
Square Footage: 2,757
Bedrooms: 4
Bathrooms: 2½
Width: 69' - 6"
Depth: 68' - 8"
Foundation: Unfinished Basement,
Slab, Crawlspace

SEARCH ONLINE @ EPLANS.COM

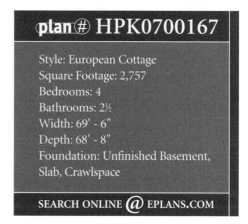

French Country appointments give this home an elegant Old World look. The foyer opens to the well-proportioned dining room, with a 12-foot ceiling. A stairway is conveniently located to provide access to the optional basement below and the attic above. Double sets of French doors with transoms open to the rear porch. Three additional bedrooms include a flex room that easily converts to a home office or study.

plan# HPK0700168

Style: European Cottage
Square Footage: 1,882
Bedrooms: 3
Bathrooms: 2½
Width: 42' - 8"
Depth: 72' - 0"
Foundation: Unfinished Basement

SEARCH ONLINE @ EPLANS.COM

Harmonizing natural elements, stone and woodwork, add the right touch to this country European design. The flexibility of a single-level home gives the convenience of a home that can age well and still meet all your needs in the coming years. Bedrooms can be repurposed as den or office space or as guest suites as needed. A large master suite with a lovely tray ceiling provides a well-lit sitting bay, roomy super bath with dual sinks, and a walk-in closet. Living spaces work in combination to afford all the openness of a modern floor plan. The spacious living room sits just off the bayed dining room and island kitchen. A fully equipped laundry room also features a powder room.

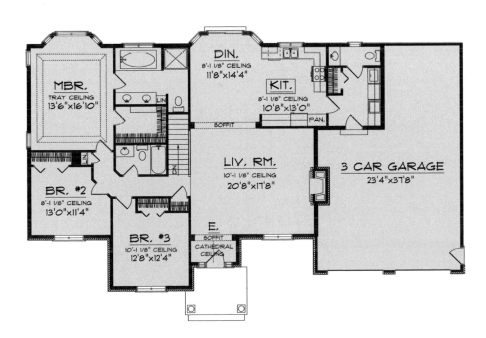

With more than 50 years of experience in the industry and millions of blueprints sold, Hanley Wood is a trusted source of high-quality, high-value pre-drawn home plans.

Using pre-drawn home plans is a **reliable, cost-effective way** to build your dream home, and our vast selection of plans is second-to-none. The nation's finest designers craft these plans that builders know they can trust. Meanwhile, our friendly, knowledgeable customer service representatives can help you every step of the way.

WHAT YOU'LL GET WITH YOUR ORDER

The contents of each designer's blueprint package is unique, but all contain detailed, high-quality working drawings. You can expect to find the following standard elements in most sets of plans:

1. FRONT PERSPECTIVE

This artist's sketch of the exterior of the house gives you an idea of how the house will look when built and landscaped.

2. FOUNDATION AND BASEMENT PLANS

This sheet shows the foundation layout including concrete walls, footings, pads, posts, beams, and bearing walls, and foundation notes. If the home features a basement, the first-floor framing details may also be included on this plan. If your plan features slab construction rather than a basement, the plan shows footings and details for a monolithic slab. This page, or another in the set, may include a sample plot plan for locating your house on a building site. Additional sheets focus on foundation cross-sections and other details.

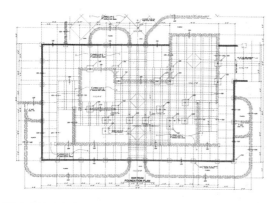

3. DETAILED FLOOR PLANS

These plans show the layout of each floor of the house. Rooms and interior spaces are carefully dimensioned, doors and windows located, and keys are given for cross-section details provided elsewhere in the plans.

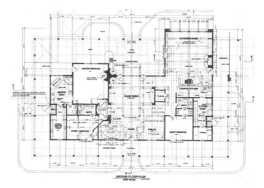

4. HOUSE AND DETAIL CROSS-SECTIONS

Large-scale views show sections or cutaways of the foundation, interior walls, exterior walls, floors, stairways, and roof details. Additional cross-sections may show important changes in floor, ceiling, or roof heights, or the relationship of one level to another. These sections show exactly how the various parts of the house fit together and are extremely valuable during construction. Additional sheets may include enlarged wall, floor, and roof construction details.

5. ROOF AND FLOOR STRUCTURAL SUPPORTS

The roof and floor framing plans provide detail for these crucial elements of your home. Each includes floor joist, ceiling joist, rafter and roof joist size, spacing, direction, span, and specifications. Beam and window headers, along with necessary details for framing connections, stairways, skylights, or dormers are also included.

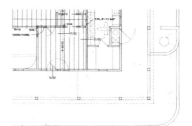

6. ELECTRICAL PLAN

The electrical plan offers a detailed outline of all wiring for your home, with notes for all lighting, outlets, switches, and circuits. A layout is provided for each level, as well as basements, garages, or other structures.

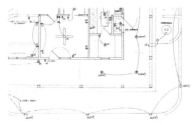

7. EXTERIOR ELEVATIONS

In addition to the front exterior, your blueprint set will include drawings of the rear and sides of your house as well. These drawings give notes on exterior materials and finishes. Particular attention is given to cornice detail, brick and stone accents, or other finish items that make your home unique.

BEFORE YOU CALL

You are making a terrific decision to use a pre-drawn house plan—it is one you can make with confidence, knowing that your blueprints are crafted by national-award-winning certified residential designers and architects, and trusted by builders.

Once you've selected the plan you want—or even if you have questions along the way—our experienced customer service representatives are available 24 hours a day, seven days a week to help you navigate the home-building process. To help them provide you with even better service, please consider the following questions before you call:

■ Have you chosen or purchased your lot?
If so, please review the building setback requirements of your local building authority before you call. You don't need to have a lot before ordering plans, but if you own land already, please have the width and depth dimensions handy when you call.

■ Have you chosen a builder?
Involving your builder in the plan selection and evaluation process may be beneficial. Luckily, builders know they can have confidence with pre-drawn plans because they've been designed for livability, functionality, and typically are builder-proven at successful home sites across the country.

■ Do you need a construction loan?
Construction loans are unique because they involve determining the value of something that is not yet constructed. Several lenders offer convenient construction-to-permanent loans. It is important to choose a good lending partner—one who will help guide you through the application and appraisal process. Most will even help you evaluate your contractor to ensure reliability and credit worthiness. Our partnership with IndyMac Bank, a nationwide leader in construction loans, can help you save on your loan, if needed (see the next page for details).

■ How many sets of plans do you need?
Building a home can typically require a number of sets of blueprints—one for yourself, two or three for the builder and subcontractors, two for the local building department, and one or more for your lender. For this reason, we offer 5- and 8-set plan packages, but your best value is the Reproducible Plan Package. Reproducible plans are accompanied by a license to make modifications and typically up to 12 duplicates of the plan so you have enough copies of the plan for everyone involved in the financing and construction of your home.

■ Do you want to make any changes to the plan?
We understand that it is difficult to find blueprints for a home that will meet all of your needs. That is why Hanley Wood is glad to offer plan Customization Services. We will work with you to design the modifications you'd like to see and to adjust your blueprint plans accordingly—anything from changing the foundation; adding square footage, redesigning baths, kitchens, or bedrooms; or most other modifications. This simple, cost-effective service saves you from hiring an outside architect to make alterations. Modifications may only be made to Reproducible Plan Packages that include the license to modify.

■ Do you have to make any changes to meet local building codes?
While all of our plans are drawn to meet national building codes at the time they were created, many areas required that plans be stamped by a local engineer to certify that they meet local building codes. Building codes are updated frequently and can vary by state, county, city, or municipality. Contact your local building inspection department, office of planning and zoning, or department of permits to determine how your local codes will affect your construction project. The best way to assure that you can make changes to your plan, if necessary, is to purchase a Reproducible Plan Package.

■ Has everyone—from family members to contractors—been involved in selecting the plan?
Building a new home is an exciting process, and using pre-drawn plans is a great way to realize your dreams. Make sure that everyone involved has had an opportunity to review the plan you've selected. While Hanley Wood is the only plans provider with an exchange policy, it's best to be sure all parties agree on your selection before you buy.

CALL TOLL-FREE 1-800-521-6797

Source Key
HPK07

CUSTOMIZE YOUR PLAN – HANLEY WOOD CUSTOMIZATION SERVICES

Creating custom home plans has never been easier and more directly accessible. Using state-of-the-art technology and top-performing architectural expertise, Hanley Wood delivers on a long-standing customer commitment to provide world-class home-plans and customization services. Our valued customers—professional home builders and individual home owners—appreciate the convenience and accessibility of this interactive, consultative service.

With the Hanley Wood Customization Service you can:
■ Save valuable time by avoiding drawn-out and frequently repetitive face-to-face design meetings
■ Communicate design and home-plan changes faster and more efficiently
■ Speed-up project turn-around time
■ Build on a budget without sacrificing quality
■ Transform master home plans to suit your design needs and unique personal style

All of our design options and prices are impressively affordable. A detailed quote is available for a $50 consultation fee. Plan modification is an interactive service. Our skilled team of designers will guide you through the customization process from start to finish making recommendations, offering ideas, and determining the feasibility of your changes. This level of service is offered to ensure the final modified plan meets your expectations. If you use our service the $50 fee will be applied to the cost of the modifications.

You may purchase the customization consultation before or after purchasing a plan. In either case, it is necessary to purchase the Reproducible Plan Package and complete the accompanying license to modify the plan before we can begin customization.

Customization Consultation $50

TOOLS TO WORK WITH YOUR BUILDER

Two Reverse Options For Your Convenience – Mirror and Right-Reading Reverse (as available)
Mirror reverse plans simply flip the design 180 degrees—keep in mind, the text will also be flipped. For a minimal fee you can have one or all of your plans shipped mirror reverse, although we recommend having at least one regular set handy. Right-reading reverse plans show the design flipped 180 degrees but the text reads normally. When you choose this option, we ship each set of purchased blueprints in this format.

Mirror Reverse Fee (indicate the number of sets when ordering) $55
Right Reading Reverse Fee (all sets are reversed) $175

A Shopping List Exclusively for Your Home – Materials List
A customized Materials List helps you plan and estimate the cost of your new home, outlining the quantity, type, and size of materials needed to build your house (with the exception of mechanical system items). Included are framing lumber, windows and doors, kitchen and bath cabinetry, rough and finished hardware, and much more.

Materials List . . . .$75 each
Additional Materials Lists (at original time of purchase only)$20 each

Plan Your Home-Building Process – Specification Outline
Work with your builder on this step-by-step chronicle of 166 stages or items crucial to the building process. It provides a comprehensive review of the construction process and helps you choose materials.
Specification Outline . . . .$10 each

Get Accurate Cost Estimates for Your Home – Quote One® Cost Reports
The Summary Cost Report, the first element in the Quote One® package, breaks down the cost of your home into various categories based on building materials, labor, and installation, and includes three grades of construction: Budget, Standard, and Custom. Make even more informed decisions about your project with the second element of our package, the Material Cost Report. The material and installation cost is shown for each of more than 1,000 line items provided in the standard-grade Materials List, which is included with this tool. Additional space is included for estimates from contractors and subcontractors, such as for mechanical materials, which are not included in our packages.

Quote One® Summary Cost Report $35
Quote One® Detailed Material Cost Report $140*
***Detailed material cost report includes the Materials List**

Learn the Basics of Building – Electrical, Pluming, Mechanical, Construction Detail Sheets
If you want to know more about building techniques—and deal more confidently with your subcontractors—we offer four useful detail sheets. These sheets provide non-plan-specific general information, but are excellent tools that will add to your understanding of Plumbing Details, Electrical Details, Construction Details, and Mechanical Details.

Electrical Detail Sheet $14.95
Plumbing Detail Sheet $14.95
Mechanical Detail Sheet $14.95
Construction Detail Sheet $14.95
SUPER VALUE SETS:
Buy any 2: $26.95; Buy any 3: $34.95; Buy All 4: $39.95

Best Value

MAKE YOUR HOME TECH-READY – HOME AUTOMATION UPGRADE

Building a new home provides a unique opportunity to wire it with a plan for future needs. A Home Automation-Ready (HA-Ready) home contains the wiring substructure of tomorrow's connected home. It means that every room—from the front porch to the backyard, and from the attic to the basement—is wired for security, lighting, telecommunications, climate control, home computer networking, whole-house audio, home theater, shade control, video surveillance, entry access control, and yes, video gaming electronic solutions.

Along with the conveniences HA-Ready homes provide, they also have a higher resale value. The Consumer Electronics Association (CEA), in conjunction with the Custom Electronic Design and Installation Association (CEDIA), have developed a TechHome™ Rating system that quantifies the value of HA-Ready homes. The rating system is gaining widespread recognition in the real estate industry.

Developed by CEDIA-certified installers, our Home Automation Upgrade package includes everything you need to work with an installer during the construction of your home. It provides a short explanation of the various subsystems, a wiring floor plan for each level of your home, a detailed materials list with estimated costs, and a list of CEDIA-certified installers in your local area.

Home Automation Upgrade $250

GET YOUR HOME PLANS PAID FOR!

IndyMac Bank, in partnership with Hanley Wood, will reimburse you up to $600 toward the cost of your home plans simply by financing the construction of your new home with IndyMac Bank Home Construction Lending.

IndyMac's construction and permanent loan is a one-time close loan, meaning that one application—and one set of closing fees—provides all the financing you need.

Apply today at www.indymacbank.com, call toll free at 1-866-237-3478, or ask a Hanley Wood customer service representative for details.

DESIGN YOUR HOME – INTERIOR AND EXTERIOR FINISHING TOUCHES

Be Your Own Interior Designer! – Home Furniture Planner

Effectively plan the space in your home using our Hands-On Home Furniture Planner. It's fun and easy—no more moving heavy pieces of furniture to see how the room will go together. The kit includes reusable peel-and-stick furniture templates that fit on a 12"x18" laminated layout board—enough space to lay out every room in your house.

Home Furniture Planning Kit $15.95

Enjoy the Outdoors! – Deck Plans

Many of our homes have a corresponding deck plan, sold separately, which includes a Deck Plan Frontal Sheet, Deck Framing and Floor Plans, Deck Elevations, and a Deck Materials List. A Standard Deck Details Package, also available, provides all the how-to information necessary for building any deck. Get both the Deck Plan and the Standard Deck Details Package for one low price in our Complete Deck Building Package. See the price tier chart below and call for deck plan availability.

Deck Details (only) $14.95
Deck Building Package . . . . Plan price + $14.95

Create a Professionally Designed Landscape – Landscape Plans

Many of our homes have a front-yard Landscape Plan that is complementary in design to the house plan. These comprehensive Landscape Blueprint Packages include a Frontal Sheet, Plan View, Regionalized Plant & Materials List, a sheet on Planting and Maintaining Your Landscape, Zone Maps, and a Plant Size and Description Guide. Each set of blueprints is a full 18" x 24" with clear, complete instructions in easy-to-read type. Our Landscape Plans are available with a Plant & Materials List adapted by horticultural experts to eight regions of the country. Please specify your region when ordering your plan—see region map below. Call for more information about landscape plan availability and applicable regions.

LANDSCAPE & DECK PRICE SCHEDULE

PRICE TIERS	1-SET STUDY PACKAGE	5-SET BUILDING PACKAGE	8-SET BUILDING PACKAGE	1-SET REPRODUCIBLE*
P1	$25	$55	$95	$145
P2	$45	$75	$115	$165
P3	$75	$105	$145	$195
P4	$105	$135	$175	$225
P5	$145	$175	$215	$275
P6	$185	$215	$255	$315

PRICES SUBJECT TO CHANGE   * REQUIRES A FAX NUMBER

TERMS & CONDITIONS

OUR EXCHANGE POLICY

HANLEY WOOD EXCLUSIVE!

Hanley Wood is committed to ensuring your satisfaction with your blueprint order, which is why we're the only provider of pre-drawn house plans to offer an exchange policy. With the exception of Reproducible Plan Package orders, we will exchange your entire first order for an equal or greater number of blueprints from our plan collection within 90 days of the original order. The entire content of your original order must be returned before an exchange will be processed. Please call our customer service department at 1-888-690-1116 for your return authorization number and shipping instructions. If the returned blueprints look used, redlined, or copied, we will not honor your exchange. Fees for exchanging your blueprints are as follows: 20% of the amount of the original order, plus the difference in cost if exchanging for a design in a higher price bracket or less the difference in cost if exchanging for a design in a lower price bracket. (Because they can be copied, Reproducible blueprints are not exchangeable or refundable.) Please call for current postage and handling prices. Shipping and handling charges are not refundable.

ARCHITECTURAL AND ENGINEERING SEALS

Some cities and states now require that a licensed architect or engineer review and "seal" a blueprint, or officially approve it, prior to construction. Prior to application for a building permit or the start of actual construction, we strongly advise that you consult your local building official who can tell you if such a review is required.

LOCAL BUILDING CODES AND ZONING REQUIREMENTS

Each plan was designed to meet or exceed the requirements of a nationally recognized model building code in effect at the time and place the plan was drawn. Typically plans designed after the year 2000 conform to the International Residential Building Code (IRC 2000 or 2003). The IRC is comprised of portions of the three major codes below. Plans drawn before 2000 conform to one of the three recognized building codes in effect at the time: Building Officials and Code Administrators (BOCA) International, Inc.; the Southern Building Code Congress International, (SBCCI) Inc.; the International Conference of Building Officials (ICBO); or the Council of American Building Officials (CABO).

Because of the great differences in geography and climate throughout the United States and Canada, each state, county, and municipality has its own building codes, zone requirements, ordinances, and building regulations. Your plan may need to be modified to comply with local requirements. In addition, you may need to obtain permits or inspections from local governments before and in the course of construction. We authorize the use of the blueprints on the express condition that you consult a local licensed architect or engineer of your choice prior to beginning construction and strictly comply with all local building codes, zoning requirements, and other applicable laws, regulations, ordinances, and requirements. Notice: Plans for homes to be built in Nevada must be redrawn by a Nevada-registered professional. Consult your local building official for more information on this subject.

TERMS AND CONDITIONS

These designs are protected under the terms of United States Copyright Law and may not be copied or reproduced in any way, by any means, unless you have purchased a Reproducible Plan Package and signed the accompanying license to modify and copy the plan, which clearly indicates your right to modify, copy, or reproduce. We authorize the use of your chosen design as an aid in the construction of ONE (1) single- or multi-family home only. You may not use this design to build a second dwelling or multiple dwellings without purchasing another blueprint or blueprints or paying additional design fees. Multi-use fees vary by designer—please call one of experienced sales representatives for a quote.

DISCLAIMER

The designers we work with have put substantial care and effort into the creation of their blueprints. However, because we cannot provide on-site consultation, supervision, and control over actual construction, and because of the great variance in local building requirements, building practices, and soil, seismic, weather, and other conditions, WE MAKE NO WARRANTY OF ANY KIND, EXPRESS OR IMPLIED, WITH RESPECT TO THE CONTENT OR USE OF THE BLUEPRINTS, INCLUDING BUT NOT LIMITED TO ANY WARRANTY OF MERCHANTABILITY OR OF FITNESS FOR A PARTICULAR PURPOSE. ITEMS, PRICES, TERMS, AND CONDITIONS ARE SUBJECT TO CHANGE WITHOUT NOTICE.

**CALL TOLL-FREE
1-866-473-4052
OR VISIT
EPLANS.COM**

IMPORTANT COPYRIGHT NOTICE

From the Council of Publishing Home Designers

BLUEPRINT PRICE SCHEDULE

PRICE TIERS	1-SET STUDY PACKAGE	5-SET BUILDING PACKAGE	8-SET BUILDING PACKAGE	1-SET REPRODUCIBLE*
A1	$450	$500	$555	$675
A2	$490	$545	$595	$735
A3	$540	$605	$665	$820
A4	$590	$660	$725	$895
C1	$640	$715	$775	$950
C2	$690	$760	$820	$1025
C3	$735	$810	$875	$1100
C4	$785	$860	$925	$1175
L1	$895	$990	$1075	$1335
L2	$970	$1065	$1150	$1455
L3	$1075	$1175	$1270	$1600
L4	$1185	$1295	$1385	$1775
SQ1				.40/SQ. FT.
SQ3				.55/SQ. FT.
SQ5				.80/SQ. FT.

PRICES SUBJECT TO CHANGE

* REQUIRES A FAX NUMBER

PLAN #	PRICE TIER	PAGE	MATERIALS LIST	QUOTE ONE®	DECK	DECK PRICE	LANDSCAPE	LANDSCAPE PRICE	REGIONS
HPK0700001	SQ1	6							
HPK0700002	SQ1	8	Y						
HPK0700003	A4	12							
HPK0700004	A4	13	Y						
HPK0700005	C2	14	Y						
HPK0700006	C3	15	Y						
HPK0700007	C3	16	Y						
HPK0700008	C1	17	Y	Y					
HPK0700009	C2	18	Y						
HPK0700010	C3	19	Y	Y			OLA024	P4	123568
HPK0700011	C4	20							
HPK0700012	C2	21	Y	Y	ODA012	P3	OLA024	P4	123568
HPK0700013	C3	22	Y						
HPK0700014	C3	23							
HPK0700015	C1	24	Y		ODA012	P3	OLA010	P3	1234568
HPK0700016	C1	25							
HPK0700017	C3	26							
HPK0700018	C3	27							
HPK0700019	C1	28	Y						
HPK0700020	C2	29	Y						
HPK0700021	C1	30							
HPK0700022	C2	31							
HPK0700023	SQ1	32	Y						
HPK0700024	C2	33							
HPK0700025	SQ1	34							
HPK0700026	C2	35							
HPK0700027	C4	36							
HPK0700028	C1	37	Y						
HPK0700029	A3	38							

PLAN #	PRICE TIER	PAGE	MATERIALS LIST	QUOTE ONE®	DECK	DECK PRICE	LANDSCAPE	LANDSCAPE PRICE	REGIONS
HPK0700030	A4	39							
HPK0700031	C1	40							
HPK0700032	A4	41							
HPK0700033	L1	42	Y						
HPK0700034	C3	43							
HPK0700035	A2	44	Y						
HPK0700036	A4	45	Y						
HPK0700037	A3	46							
HPK0700038	A3	47							
HPK0700039	A4	48	Y						
HPK0700040	A3	49	Y						
HPK0700041	C2	50							
HPK0700042	A4	52							
HPK0700043	SQ1	53	Y	Y					
HPK0700044	C3	54							
HPK0700045	L2	55							
HPK0700046	C1	56							
HPK0700047	A4	57	Y						
HPK0700048	A3	58							
HPK0700049	C3	59							
HPK0700050	SQ1	60							
HPK0700051	SQ1	61							
HPK0700052	C3	62							
HPK0700053	C3	63							
HPK0700054	C3	64							
HPK0700055	SQ1	65	Y						
HPK0700056	C2	66							
HPK0700057	SQ1	67							
HPK0700058	C2	68							

PLAN #	PRICE TIER	PAGE	MATERIALS LIST	QUOTE ONE®	DECK	DECK PRICE	LANDSCAPE	LANDSCAPE PRICE	REGIONS
HPK0700059	C4	69							
HPK0700060	CI	70							
HPK0700061	CI	71							
HPK0700062	CI	72							
HPK0700063	SQI	73							
HPK0700064	CI	74							
HPK0700065	A4	75	Y						
HPK0700066	CI	76							
HPK0700067	A2	77	Y						
HPK0700068	C3	78							
HPK0700069	C2	79							
HPK0700070	A4	80	Y	Y	ODA012	P3	OLA083	P3	12345678
HPK0700071	A2	81	Y						
HPK0700072	CI	82							
HPK0700073	AI	84	Y						
HPK0700074	C2	85							
HPK0700075	A2	86							
HPK0700076	C2	87							
HPK0700077	A4	88							
HPK0700078	A2	89	Y						
HPK0700079	A3	90	Y						
HPK0700080	A2	91	Y						
HPK0700081	A2	92							
HPK0700082	CI	93							
HPK0700083	A4	94	Y						
HPK0700084	A4	95	Y						
HPK0700085	A4	96	Y						
HPK0700086	A4	97	Y						
HPK0700087	A3	98	Y						
HPK0700088	A4	99	Y						
HPK0700089	A2	100							
HPK0700090	A2	101	Y						
HPK0700091	CI	102	Y						
HPK0700092	A3	103							
HPK0700093	CI	104							
HPK0700094	A2	105	Y						
HPK0700095	CI	106							
HPK0700096	A4	107							
HPK0700097	A2	108	Y						
HPK0700098	A4	109	Y						
HPK0700099	A4	110							
HPK0700100	A2	111							
HPK0700101	A3	112	Y						
HPK0700102	C2	113							
HPK0700103	A4	114	Y						
HPK0700104	A3	115	Y						
HPK0700105	C2	116							
HPK0700106	A3	118							
HPK0700107	A4	119							
HPK0700108	SQI	120	Y		ODA011	P2	OLA024	P4	123568
HPK0700109	C4	121							
HPK0700110	C4	122							
HPK0700111	SQI	123							
HPK0700112	CI	124	Y						
HPK0700113	C4	125							
HPK0700114	SQI	126							
HPK0700115	C4	127	Y	Y	ODA012	P3	OLA024	P4	123568
HPK0700116	A4	128	Y						
HPK0700117	A4	129	Y		ODA011	P2	OLA025	P3	123568
HPK0700118	A4	130	Y						
HPK0700119	A4	131	Y						
HPK0700120	C3	132							
HPK0700121	CI	133							
HPK0700122	CI	134							
HPK0700123	C3	135	Y	Y			OLA024	P4	123568
HPK0700124	SQI	136					OLA010	P3	1234568
HPK0700125	CI	137							
HPK0700126	SQI	138	Y		ODA011	P2	OLA088	P4	12345678
HPK0700127	CI	139	Y						
HPK0700128	A4	140							
HPK0700129	CI	141	Y						
HPK0700130	CI	142							
HPK0700131	CI	143							
HPK0700132	C2	144							
HPK0700133	C2	145							
HPK0700134	A3	146	Y						
HPK0700135	CI	147	Y	Y					
HPK0700136	A3	148	Y						
HPK0700137	A3	149	Y						
HPK0700138	A4	150	Y						
HPK0700139	A4	151	Y						
HPK0700140	A3	152							
HPK0700141	A4	154							
HPK0700142	CI	155	Y						
HPK0700143	C3	156							
HPK0700144	A3	157							
HPK0700145	C2	158							
HPK0700146	C2	159	Y	Y					
HPK0700147	A2	160	Y						
HPK0700148	CI	161							
HPK0700149	AI	162	Y						
HPK0700150	C2	163	Y						
HPK0700151	A4	164							
HPK0700152	A3	165							
HPK0700153	A2	166	Y						
HPK0700154	A2	167	Y						
HPK0700155	C3	168	Y						
HPK0700156	SQI	169							
HPK0700157	C2	170	Y						
HPK0700158	C2	171							
HPK0700159	CI	172	Y						
HPK0700160	CI	173	Y						
HPK0700161	A3	174							
HPK0700162	C4	175							
HPK0700163	CI	176							
HPK0700164	CI	177							
HPK0700165	A4	178							
HPK0700166	CI	179							
HPK0700167	CI	180							
HPK0700168	A3	181							

Turn Your Dream Home Into A *Reality*

ARTS & CRAFTS HOME PLANS
1-931131-26-0

$14.95 (128 PAGES)
This title showcases 85 home plans in the Craftsman, Prairie and Bungalow styles.

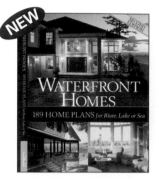

NEW

WATERFRONT HOMES
1-931131-28-7

$10.95 (208 PAGES)
A collection of gorgeous homes for those who dream of life on the water's edge—this title features open floor plans with expansive views.

SUN COUNTRY STYLES
1-931131-14-7

$9.95 (192 PAGES)
175 designs from Coastal Cottages to stunning Southwesterns.

Finding the right new home to fit

▶ Your style
▶ Your budget
▶ Your life

…has never been easier.

Our spring collection offers distinctive design coupled with plans to match every wallet. If you are looking to build your new home, look to HomePlanners first.

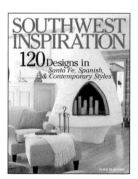

SOUTHWEST INSPIRATION
1-931131-19-8

$14.95 (192 PAGES)
This title features 120 designs in Santa Fe, Spanish and Contemporary styles.

MEDITERRANEAN INSPIRATION
1-931131-09-0

$14.95 (192 PAGES)
Bring home the timeless beauty of the Mediterranean with the gorgeous plans featured in this popular title.

FARMHOUSE & COUNTRY PLANS
1-881955-77-X

$10.95 (320 PAGES)
Farmhouse & Country Plans features 300 fresh designs from classic to modern.

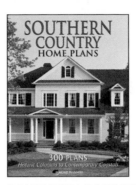

SOUTHERN COUNTRY HOME PLANS
1-931131-06-6

$10.95 (320 PAGES)
Southern Country Home Plans showcases 300 plans from Historic Colonials to Contemporary Coastals.

PROVENCAL INSPIRATION
1-881955-89-3

$14.95 (192 PAGES)
This title features home plans, landscapes and interior plans that evoke the French Country spirit.

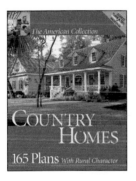

THE AMERICAN COLLECTION: COUNTRY HOMES
1-931131-35-X

$10.95 (192 PAGES)
The American Collection: Country is a must-have if you're looking to build a country home or if you want to bring the relaxed country spirit into your current home.

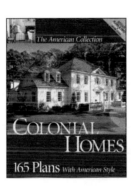

THE AMERICAN COLLECTION: COLONIAL HOMES
1-931131-40-6

$10.95 (192 PAGES)
This beautiful collection features distinctly American home styles— find everything from Colonials, Cape Cod, Georgian, Farmhouse to Saltbox.

HANLEY WOOD CONSUMER GROUP
One Thomas Circle, NW, Suite 600, Washington, DC 20005

AC2

Well-designed country homes let you leave your cares behind. Here, there's plenty of room to relax, whether it's outdoors on one of the verandas or in the media room that occupies the turret on the first floor. For details on Design HPK0700111, see page 123.